M2 MACBOO: 13-INCH) USER GUIDE

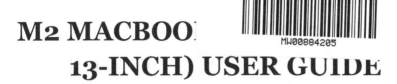

A Complete Step By Step Instruction Manual for Beginners and seniors to Learn How to Use the New M2 Chip MacBook Air Like A Pro With MacOS Tips & Tricks

BY

HERBERT A. CLARK

Table of Contents

INTRODUCTION.. 1

WHAT'S IN THE BOX 2

FEATURES OF THE M2 MACBOOK AIR 3

Design..3

Touch ID...5

Display...6

Storage & Memory..7

Battery Life 7

SETUP YOUR DEVICE 8

KNOW YOUR WAY AROUND.............................. 15

The Desktop & menu bar on your MacBook 15

Change Menu bar settings.. 17

Finder on Mac 20

The Dock 22

Perform other actions for items in the Dock................... 24

Customize the Dock... 25

Notification Center 27

Control Centre... 31

Use the Controls Centre 32

Personalize the Controls Centre...................................... 33

System Settings 35

Set Options 35

Find options in Systems Settings 37

Update macOS. 37

Spotlight on your Mac 38

Launchpad...40

Open & close the Launchpad.. 41

Find & launch applications in Launchpad 41

Organize applications in Launchpad.............................. 42

Remove applications from Launchpad 42

Apple ID 43

MacBook Air trackpad.....................................45

BASIC SETTINGS 50

Shut down your device 50

Restart your MacBook....................................... 51

Put your device to sleep or wake it 51

Put your device to sleep 52

Wake your device from sleep 52

Connect your device to the Internet 52

Use WiFi.. 53

Connect with Ethernet 55

Use an iPad or iPhone to connect your MacBook to the internet . 57

View & edit files with Quick Look 59

Take a screenshot or record your Mac's screen.. 61

Take a photo or screen recording using Screenshot 62

Use keyboard shortcuts to capture screenshots 64

Change the brightness of your Mac screen 65

Use the brightness key 65

Adjust the brightness automatically 66

Adjust the brightness manually 67

Increase or decrease your MacBook's volume 67

Launch applications on your device 69

Manage application windows on your MacBook 70

Move, align, & merge application windows 71

Minimize or maximize application windows 73

Quickly switch between application windows 74

Close one or all windows for an application 74

Use applications in full screen 75

Use applications in Split View 76

Personalize the desktop photo 80

Use light or dark mode on your Mac 84

Change Night Shift settings 85

Use a screen saver 87

Personalize the screen saver on your MacBook 88

Start or stop the screen saver on your device 89

Require a password when you wake your MacBook 90

Change a user's login photo.............................90

Set your MacBook to log out when you are not using it..95

Change your Mac's login password 96

Reset your MacBook login passcode using your Apple ID 97

Create Memoji in Messages...............................99

Change the language your MacBook uses 100

Change the system language.. 101

Choose the language for each application 101

Make everything on your display bigger 102

Change text size..104

Change the size of icons 106

Control camera access on Mac 107

Use the desktop stacks 108

Activate desktop stacks.. 109

View the files in a stack 110

Expand or collapse a desktop stack.............................. 111

Change the grouping of stacks on the desktop............ 111

Uninstall applications 112

Use Hot Corners..112

Use Live Text to interact with text in pictures...115

Start a Quick Note 118

STAGE MANAGER 119

Enable or disable Stage Manager 120

Use Stage Manager.. 122

Display or hide Stage Manager in the menu bar
.... 123

Change Stage Manager settings 124

TOUCH ID 127

Set up Touch ID... 127

Rename or delete fingerprints.......................... 129

Use Touch ID to unlock, sign in, or change users
on your Mac...131

SIRI 132

Activate Siri 133

Summon Siri... 136

Deactivate Siri 137

Clear Siri & Dictation history 137

If Siri isn't working as expected 138

KEYBOARD SHORTCUTS.....................................140

Learn macOS keyboard shortcuts 141

Personalize keyboard shortcuts....................... 142

Turn off keyboard shortcuts 146

Default keyboard shortcuts 147

Copy, paste, cute, and some other common shortcuts 147

Documents shortcuts 149

System and finder shortcut 150

FACETIME.. 153

Sign in to FaceTime.. 153

Stop receiving FaceTime calls 153

Make a FaceTime call on your Mac 155

Make a group Face-Time call 157

Add others to a FaceTime call 159

Pause a Face-Time video call............................. 160

End a call 160

Accept FaceTime calls 161

Reject a Face-Time call..................................... 162

Return recent or missed calls from Face-Time 163

Return a call in another way............................. 164

Create & share a Face-Time link 164

Start a FaceTime call from the link 165

Allow callers to join Face-Time calls 165

Delete a Face-Time link..................................... 166

Join a call on your MacBook from a Face-Time link.. 167

Join a call on a Windows or Android device from a Face-Time link 168

Manage FaceTime calls on the web 168

Use SharePlay to share your screen on FaceTime 170

Take Live Photos on FaceTime 171

Setup FaceTime for Live Pictures 171

Setup Photos For Live Photos 172

Capture a Live Photo 172

Mute or change FaceTime call volume 172

Filter out background sounds 173

Enable or disable Portrait mode 175

Activate Live Captions in FaceTime 176

Change or turn off all notifications from Face-Time 176

Change FaceTime ringtones 177

Block FaceTime callers 177

Delete your FaceTime call history 178

Keyboard shortcuts in FaceTime 178

MAIL 180

Add an email account in Mail 180

Sign out of or temporarily disable an e-mail account 181

Sign out or remove an email account 181

Write & send an email 182

Schedule an email with the Send Later feature 184

Unsend e-mails with Undo Send...................... 185

Add pictures & other files in e-mails 186

Reply or forward e-mails.................................. 186

Use Remind Me to come back to e-mails later . 187

View e-mail attachments.................................. 189

Save e-mail attachments 190

Delete attachments.. 190

Delete an e-mail 190

Search for emails...191

Use Mail Privacy Protection 192

SAFARI 193

Visit a site using Safari 193

Bookmark sites you would like to revisit.......... 195

Add a bookmark 195

Find your bookmarks... 195

Use a bookmark... 197

Manage bookmarks.. 197

Use tabs 197

Open a new tab 198

Preview a tab..198

Open a web page in a new tab................................199

Open a tab in another window................................199

Reopen a recently closed tab................................199

Hide advertisements when reading text in Safari
....199

View articles using Reader....................................200

Change how webpages look in Reader....................200

Translate a webpage...201

Check the items you've downloaded 201

Save a picture from a website..........................201

Interact with the text in an image 202

Allow or block pop-ups in Safari 203

Block or allow pop-ups on a site.............................204

Block or allow pop-ups on all sites.........................205

Clear your browsing history 207

Private browsing..207

APPLE PAY 209

Add a credit or debit card for Apple Pay 209

Use Apple Pay to pay for items online or in
applications 210

Change your default card 212

Remove a card 212

Update your Apple Pay billing info 212

Update your Apple Pay contact info 213

VOICE MEMOS 214

USE YOUR MACBOOK WITH OTHER APPLE
DEVICES.. 217

Handoff 217

Enable or disable Handoff 218

Hand off between devices... 219

Universal Clipboard 221

Enable or disable Handoff 222

Use Universal Clipboard 223

Sidecar 224

Setup Sidecar 225

Change sidecar options 226

Use Sidecar 227

Use your iPhone as a webcam on your MacBook
....229

Mount your iPhone... 230

Select an external camera on your Mac........................ 231

Use your iPhone as a microphone or webcam............... 232

Activate Video Effects.. 232

If you can't find your phone as a Mic or camera option 234

Upload pictures & scans with Continuity Camera
....235

Capture a picture 236

Scan documents 238

AirDrop.. 241

Send items via AirDrop 242

Get things using AirDrop 243

Let others send things to your MacBook via AirDrop 244

Use Control Centre to manage AirDrop 245

INDEX.. 247

INTRODUCTION

Apple now sells two models of the M2 MacBook Air, one is a 13" device and the other measures in at 15". The 13-inch model was released in 2022, while the 15" model was released in June 2023. The MacBook Air now has a redesigned chassis that ditches the old design and it has the same design as the MacBook Pro.

These devices are the best laptops for individuals who want to spend some money on a great laptop. They offer great performance, more than Fifteen hours of battery life, & a bright & colourful display in a sleek and portable design.

WHAT'S IN THE BOX

15-inch MacBook Air with M2 chip

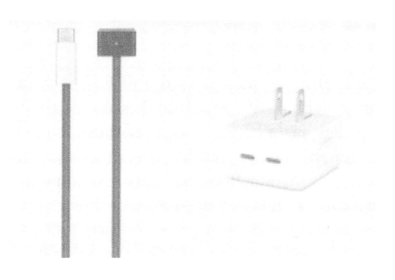

USB-C to MagSafe 3 Cable   USB-C Power Adapter
(2 m)

FEATURES OF THE M2 MACBOOK AIR

Design

Apple updated the MacBook Air's design in 2022, marking the 1st major design update to the device since 2010. The new MacBook Air ditches the tapered chassis that it has used for years, and now introduces a sleeker body that has the same thickness from back to front.

In June 2023, Apple released a new 15-inch model of the MacBook Air, which makes use of the same design but has a larger screen for those looking for an affordable device that has a big display. The 13-inch & 15-inch MacBook Air have the same design except for the chassis & screen size.

The 13-inch MacBook Air measures in at 11.30mm thick, which is slightly thinner than the previous model's thickest point (16.10mm). The device is 11.97" long, 8.46" deep & weighs 2.70 pounds, slightly lighter than the previous model.

While the 15-inch model measures in at 11.50mm thick. It's 13.4" long, 9.35" deep & weighs 3.30 pounds.

On the left side of both devices, you'll find two Thunderbolt/ USB-C ports, as well as a MagSafe charging port.

On the right side of the device, you'll find a 3.50mm headphone jack.

3.5 mm headphone jack

The MacBook Air comes in dark blue, Midnight, Starlight, Space Gray, & Silver colour options.

Touch ID

Touch ID
(power button)

The device has a Touch ID fingerprint sensor near the Fn buttons on top of the keyboard. The Touch ID is powered by a secure Enclave which can help to protect your data & personal info.

You can use the Touch ID to unlock your device by simply placing your finger on the sensor. It can also replace passwords for applications and can be used to authenticate Apple Pay purchases.

Display

The 13" & 15" MacBook Air have thin bezels and use "Liquid Retina Screen". The 13" MacBook Air has a resolution of 2560 by 1664 at 224 pixels per inch, while the 15" MacBook Air has a resolution of 2880 x 1864 at 224 pixels per inch. Both screens offer compatibility for one billion colours & P3 Wide colour for clear, true-to-life colours.

The MacBook Air's screen makes use of True Tone, which is designed to change the display's colour to match the ambient lighting. True Tone uses the multi-channel ambient light sensor inside the MacBook Air to determine the ambient light and colour temperature.

After it detects the white balance, the device can change the colour & intensity of the screen to match the light if the room for a more natural viewing experience, that's pleasant to the eyes.

Storage & Memory

The MacBook Air is compatible with up to 24 GB of RAM & about 2 TB of storage space. The base model is available in 8 GB of memory & 256 GB of storage space.

Battery Life

The 13" model has a 52.60-watt lithium-polymer battery, while the 15" model has a 66.50-watt lithium-polymer battery that can last about Eighteen hours when watching videos on the Apple TV application or about Fifteen hours when surfing the internet.

SETUP YOUR DEVICE

When your switch on your device for the first time, Set up Assistant would walk you through the simple steps you need to get started with your new MacBook Air.

Set up Assistant would guide you through the following:

❖ Set your region or country: This determines your MacBook Air's language & time zone.

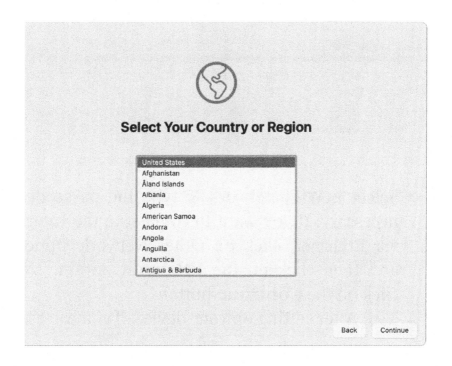

❖ Accessibility options: Checkout accessibility options for Cognitive abilities, Hearing, Vision, & Motor or click on the **Not Now** option.

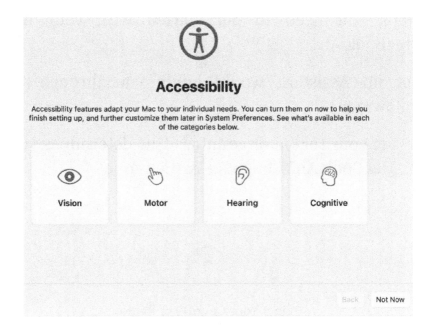

❖ Select a WiFi network & type the passcode, if necessary. If you want to connect to the Internet via Ethernet, click on Other Network Options, and then click on the **Ethernet** button. Next, click on the **Continue** button

Tip: After setting up your device, if you can't find the WiFi status icon 📶 on the menu bar, you can simply add it. Select Apple menu, click on System Settings, click on Controls Centre in the sidebar, and then select **Show in Menu Bar** for Wifi.

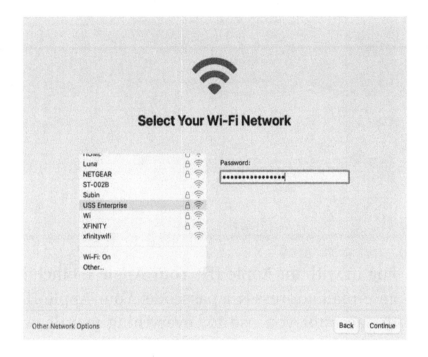

❖ Data migration: If you want to setup this device as a new device without transferring any files from your old computer, click on **Not Now** in the Migration Assistant window. In this chapter, we will be setting up your device as a new device.

Migration Assistant

If you have information on another Mac or a Windows PC, you can transfer it to this Mac. You can also transfer information from a Time Machine backup or another startup disk.

How do you want to transfer your information?

○ From a Mac, Time Machine backup or Startup disk

From a Windows PC

Not Now   Back   Continue

❖ Log in with an Apple ID: Your Apple ID includes an e-mail address & a passcode. Your Apple ID is the account you use for everything you do with Apple, which includes making use of the Apps Store, iCloud, the Apple TV application, etc. If you do not have an Apple ID, you can setup an Apple ID for yourself while setting up your MacBook Air.

Sign In with Your Apple ID

Sign in to use iCloud, the App Store, and other Apple services.

Apple ID [Email]

Create new Apple ID...

Forgot Apple ID or password?

Use different Apple IDs for iCloud and Apple media purchases?

This Mac will be associated with your Apple ID and data such as photos, contacts, and documents will be stored in iCloud so you can access them on other devices. See how your data is managed...

Set Up Later   Back   Continue

❖ Save files in iCloud: You can save your contents (images, documents, etc.) in the cloud & gain access to them wherever you are. Just make sure you are using the same Apple ID on all your Apple devices. To configure this option later, select Apple menu , click on Systems Setting and click on **Sign in your Apple ID** in the side bar if you've not already. After signing in, click on the **Apple ID** button in the side bar, click on iCloud, and then choose the features you want.

❖ Screen Time: This feature keeps track of the time you spend on your device.

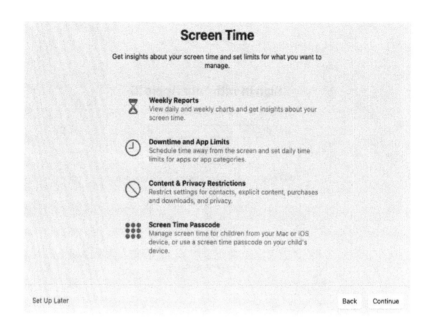

❖ Activate Siri & Hey Siri: You can activate Siri & Hey Siri while setting up your MacBook Air.

Siri

Siri helps you get things done just by asking. Siri can also make suggestions before you ask in apps, search, and keyboards.

☑ Enable Ask Siri

Apple stores transcripts of your interactions with Siri and may review a subset of these transcripts. Siri may also send information like your voice input, Hey Siri setup, contacts, and location to Apple to process your request. Data is not associated with your Apple ID.
About Ask Siri, Dictation & Privacy...

Back   Continue

❖ Configure Touch ID: You can register a finger-print to Touch ID when setting up your MacBook Air. You can use your registered fingerprint to unlock your device, sign into 3rd party applications, authenticate purchases from the iTunes Store, Apps Store, etc. & make online purchases with Apple Pay.

❖ Set up Apple Pay. You can use Apple Pay to securely pay for items when shopping online. Simply adhere to the directives on your screen to add & verify your card

❖ Pick a look: Choose Auto, Dark, or Light for your desktop appearance. If you want to change the look you selected when setting up your MacBook Air, simply select Apple menu , click on Systems Settings, click on Appearance, and then select one of the options.

KNOW YOUR WAY AROUND

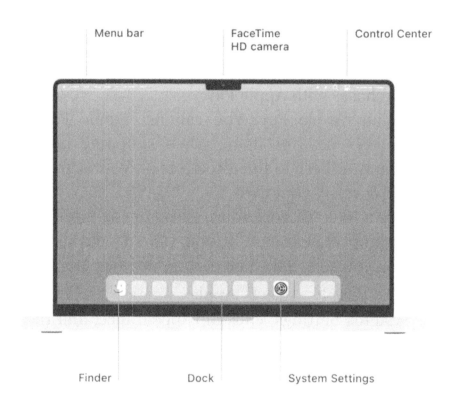

Menu bar

FaceTime
HD camera

Control Center

Finder

Dock

System Settings

The Desktop & menu bar on your MacBook

The Desktop is where you can quickly launch applications, arrange your files, search for everything on your device and the internet, etc.

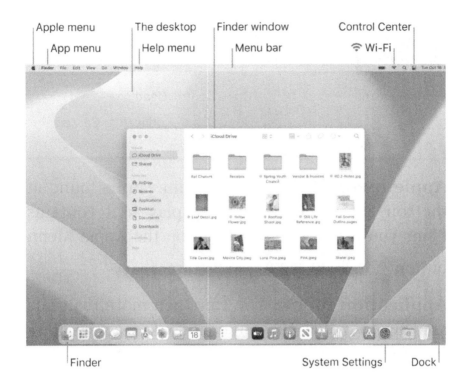

Apple menu   The desktop   Finder window   Control Center

App menu   Help menu   Menu bar   🛜 Wi-Fi

Finder   System Settings   Dock

Menu bar: The menu bar can be found at the upper part of your display. You can use the menus on the left part of the menu bar to select commands & carry out tasks in applications. The items in the menu vary depending on the application you are making use of. You can use the icons on the right part of the menu bar to connect to a WiFi network, view your WiFi status 🛜, open the Controls Centre 🎚, search with Spotlight 🔍, etc.

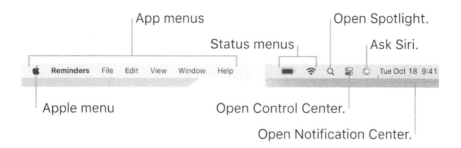

Apple menu : The Apple menu can be found at the top left corner of your display & it contains items you use frequently. Click on the Apple Menu button to open the Apple menu.

Application menu: You can open more than one app & window at the same time. The active app's name will appear in bold close to the right part of the Apple menu , followed by the application's own menus. If you launch another application or click on a different app's window, the name in the application menu will change to that application as well as the menus in the menu bar.

Change Menu bar settings

To customize the menu bar, simply adhere to the directives below:

❖ Select Apple menu , then click on Systems Settings

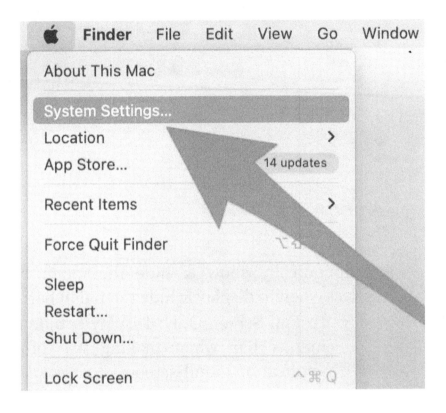

❖ Click on the Desktop and Dock button on the sidebar. (You might have to scroll down.)
❖ In the **Menu Bar** section on the right, select any of the following options to customize the settings:

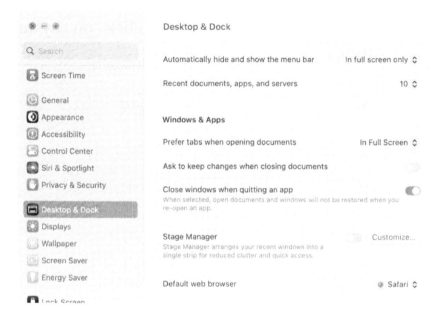

> Automatically show & hide the menu bar: select when to display & hide the menu bar:
>   • In Full Screen Only: Display & hide the menus bar when making use of an application in full-screen.
>   • Desktop only: Display & hide the menus bar when you aren't making use of an application in full screen.
>   • Never: Never conceal the menus bar
>   • Always: Always display & hide the menus bar
> Recent apps, servers, & documents: Select the number of items to display in the recent items menu. The items that you have used recently

are displayed in the Apple menu, where you can easily access them.

Finder on Mac

The Finder, represented by a smiley face with a blue icon, is the backbone of your MacBook. In the Finder, you can sort & gain access to almost everything on your MacBook, including your pictures, movies, documents, & other files on your device. Click on the Finder icon in the Dock at the lower part of your display to open a Finder window. Force-click a file icon to check out the contents of the file, or force click on a file-name to edit it

The Finder window: To change how folders & documents are displayed in the Finder, simply click on the pop-up menu icon at the upper part of the Finder window. You can view them in a gallery, in hierarchical columns, in a list, or as icons. The sidebar displays the items you use frequently or the items you want to open quickly. To view all the files you saved on iCloud Drive, click on the iCloud Drive folder in the side bar. If you want to change what is displayed in the side bar, simply select Finder> Settings.

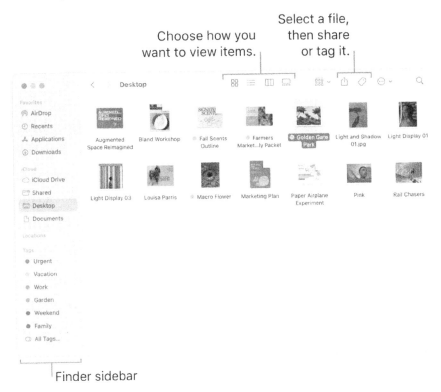

Finder sidebar

Synchronize devices. After connecting a device like an iPad or iPhone to your MacBook, it will appear in the sidebar of the Finder. Click on the name of the device to view options to update, backup, synchronize, & restore the device.

Gallery view:

Gallery View allows you to view a large preview of your file so that you can visually identify your video clips, pictures, & other documents. The Preview panel on the right displays info that can help you identify the file you want. Press Shift-Cmd-P to open or close the Preview Pane. Select View>Show Preview to display the Preview Pane options in the Finder.

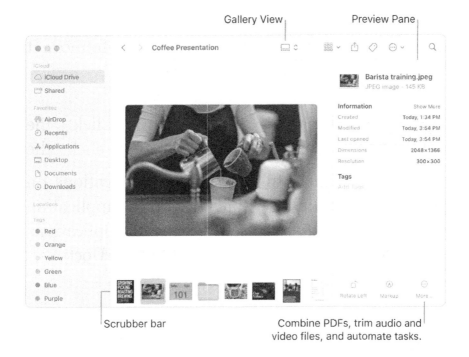

Gallery View

Preview Pane

Scrubber bar

Combine PDFs, trim audio and video files, and automate tasks.

The Dock

The Dock which can be found at the lower part of your display is a suitable place to store documents & applications you use frequently.

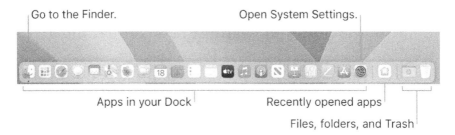

Go to the Finder.   Open System Settings.

Apps in your Dock   Recently opened apps
Files, folders, and Trash

By default, the Dock can be found at the lower part of your display, but you can set an option to move it to the right or left edge of your screen.

Open a file or application. Click the application's icon on the Dock, or click the Launchpad icon ⸬ to view all the applications on your MacBook Air, after that click on the application you want to launch. Recently opened applications can be found in the middle segment of the Dock.

Indicates an open

Close an application. You can close a window by clicking on the red dot in the upper left edge of the window (Note that an application will remain open even after you close its window). Open applications always have a dot under them in the Dock. To close an application, ctrl-click on the application icon in the Dock, then click on the **Quit** button.

Perform other actions for items in the Dock

Carry out any of the below in the Dock:

❖ View a shortcut menu of actions: Ctrl-click on an item in the dock to show its shortcut menu, then select any of the actions, or click on a file-name to open the file.
❖ Force quit an application: If an application stops responding, ctrl-click on the application's icon, then select the **Force Quit** button.

Add items to the Dock: Drag the item and drop it in the Dock. Put applications in the left segment of the Dock, & put folders or files in the right segment.

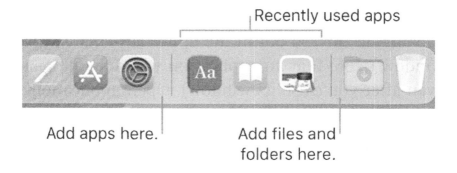

Recently used apps

Add apps here.   Add files and
                   folders here.

Remove items from the Dock: Drag the application, folder, or file out of the Dock. The item will not be removed from your device—only from the Dock.

Customize the Dock

❖ On your MacBook Air, select Apple menu > Systems Setting, then click on Desktop & Dock in the side bar.

❖ In the Dock section on the right, make changes to any of the following options:

➢ Size: Move the slider to change the size of the Dock.

➢ Magnification: Icons enlarge as you hover the cursor over them. Move the slider to select the size of the magnification.

➢ Position on the screen: Change the location of the Dock on your display. You can choose to move it to the right, bottom, or left edge of your display.

➢ Minimize windows using: Select a visual effect to use when a window is minimized.

➢ Double-click the title bar of a window: select what happens when you double-click a window's title bar

➢ Minimize windows into app icons: Minimize an application window to the application icon in the Dock. If this option is not activated, the window will be minimized to a single area in the Dock.

➢ Automatically show & hide the Dock: Hides the Dock when you are not making use of it. To reveal the hidden Dock, simply hover the cursor to the edge of your display where the Dock is located.

➢ Animate opening apps: This option makes icons bounce when you open applications.

➢ Show indicators for open applications: Display a small dot under the icon of an application when the application is open.

➢ Show recent apps in the Dock: Display the applications you've opened recently towards one end of the Dock.

Click on the Help icon ? at the lower part of the window to get more info about the options.

See everything that's open on your device.
Press the Mission Control button ⊟▢ on the keyboard to see open windows, full-screen applications, desktop spaces, etc.

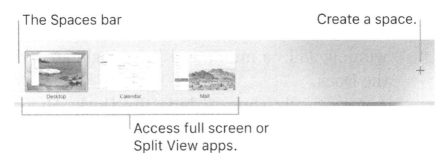

The Spaces bar   Create a space.

Desktop   Calendar   Mail

Access full screen or
Split View apps.

View all open windows in an application.
Force Click an application in the Dock to see all the application's open windows. **To Force-click, simply click then press deeper**.

Notification Center

The Notifications Centre stores all your important info, widgets, & reminders in one place. Get detailed information about calendar events, weather, etc.—

and find notifications you may have missed (reminders, messages, e-mails, etc.).

Click the date and time to open Notification Center.

See notifications you missed and keep track of your day.

Customize widgets.

Open the Notifications Centre. Click on the Time & Date at the upper right part of your display, then scroll down to see more.

Click to open
Notification Center.

Focus. When you are at work, eating dinner, or just do not want to be interrupted, the Focus feature can automatically filter your notifications so you only see the ones you specify. Focus can halt all notifications or only allow some to appear, and it can use a status in the Messages application to let your contacts know that you've silenced your notifications. To setup Focus, open Systems Setting and then click on the **Focus** button in the side bar. To activate or deactivate Focus, click on the Controls Centre icon in the menu bar, then click on the Focus segment and then select one from the Focus options.

You can set a Focus according to what you are currently doing, and you can receive notifications, phone calls, & more from certain people, etc.

Interact with your notifications. Answer an e-mail, listen to a podcast, or check the details of a calendar event. Click on the arrow in the upper right corner of a notification to see options, take action, or receive more info.

Set your notifications settings. Open Systems Setting, then click on Notifications to choose which notifications you want to see.

Customize your widget. Click on the **Edit Widgets** button (under the notifications) to add, remove, or organize widgets

Control Centre

Click an icon to turn an item on or off.

Open or close Control Center.

For some controls, click anywhere to see more options.

The Controls Centre on your device provides fast access to important macOS settings like Focus, WiFi, brightness, or volume. You can personalize the Controls Centre by adding other items, like fast user switching or accessibility shortcuts.

Use the Controls Centre

❖ On your MacBook, click on the Controls Centre icon in the menu bar.
  You will see an orange dot beside the icon indicating that your Mac's microphone is in use; you can see the application that's making use of it at the upper part of the Controls Centre
❖ Carry out any of the below with items in the Controls Centre:
  ➤ Slide the slider to decrease or increase a feature, for instance, slide the Volume slider to change your Mac's volume.
  ➤ Click on an icon to activate or deactivate a setting, for instance, click on Bluetooth or AirDrop to activate or deactivate it.
  ➤ Click on the arrow of an item to view more options, for instance, click on the **Focus** button to see your Focus list and activate or deactivate a Focus.

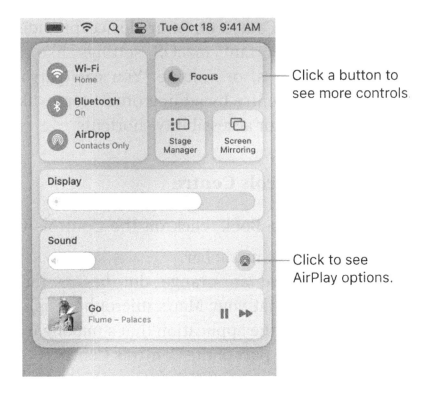

Click a button to see more controls

Click to see AirPlay options.

Personalize the Controls Centre

❖ On your MacBook, select Apple menu > Systems Setting, then click on Controls Centre in the side bar.

❖ Select the settings for items in the following segments on the right.

➢ Controls Centre Modules: Items in this segment are always displayed in the Controls Centre; you cannot remove these items from the Controls Centre. You can also decide to display these items in the menu bar. Click on the drop-down menu beside an item, then select any of the options.

➢ Other modules: You can add items from this segment to the menu bar & Controls Centre. Enable or disable each option under an item.

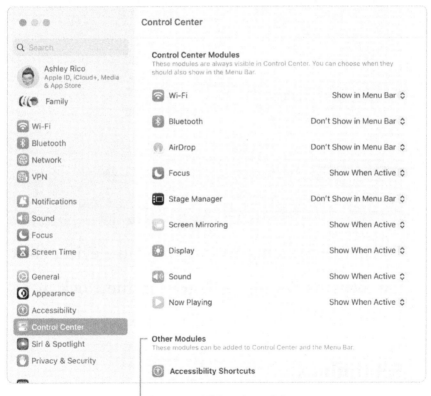

Choose additional modules to add to Control Center.

System Settings

Systems Settings is the place where you can customize your device settings. You can change your desktop wallpaper in System Settings, and more.

To change Systems Setting on your device, click on the Systems Setting button  in the Dock or select Apple menu > Systems Settings

Set Options
Your Mac's options are organized by settings. For instance, you can find customizable options for Accent Colour & Highlight Colour in the Appearance settings.

You can find all Settings in the sidebar. Click on one of the settings to see its options.

Many settings have a Help icon ⑦ that you can click to get more info about the options.

Choose options on the right.

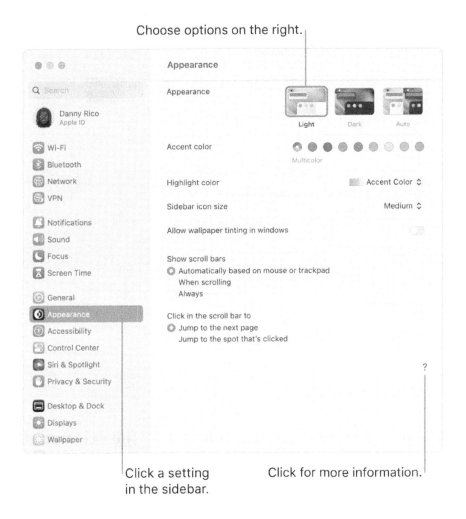

Click a setting in the sidebar.

Click for more information.

Find options in Systems Settings

If you do not know where an option is in System Settings, you can use the search box at the upper part of the window. The settings that match what you've searched for will be displayed below.

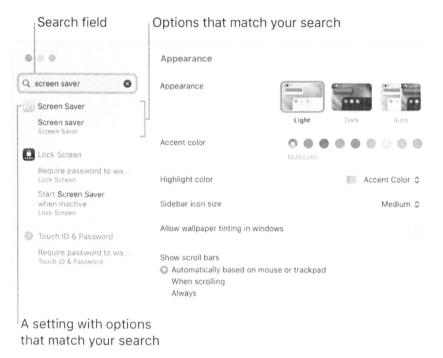

Update macOS.

Open Systems Settings, click on the **General** button and then click on the **Software Updates** option to see if your device is using the latest macOS software. You can set the option for automatic software update.

Spotlight on your Mac

With the Spotlight feature, you can easily find things on your device like photos, contacts, documents, apps etc.

Find what you want.

Start typing, and results appear quickly.

Click on the Spotlight icon  at the upper right part of your display, or press the Spotlight button (F4) on the keyboard to open Spotlight

Tip: To display or hide Spotlight's search bar simply press Cmd-Spacebar.

Open an application. Type the name of the application in Spotlight then press the **Return** button.

Perform quick actions.

Convert currencies & measurements: Type a currency, such as $, or €, and type an amount, then press the **Return** button to convert the currency. Type a measurement, like 50ft, or 30lbs, to meters.

Launchpad

Launchpad arranges your apps in a grid.
Click an app icon to open it.   Folder containing apps

Launchpad icon   App Store icon

The Launchpad is a central place where you can easily find and launch all your applications.

Click to open an app.

Drag an app over another   Click the dots or swipe
to create a folder.   to see more apps.

Open & close the Launchpad

❖ Open Launchpad: Click on the Launchpad button
   ⠿ in the Dock.
❖ Close   Launchpad   without   launching   an
   application: Press the **Esc** button.

Find & launch applications in Launchpad

* Look for an application: Type the name of the application in the search box at the upper part of the Launchpad. Or press Cmd-Right Arrow or Cmd-Left Arrow to check another page in Launchpad.
* Click on an application to open it

Organize applications in Launchpad

* Move an application by dragging it to a different location on the page.
* To move an application to a different Launchpad page, simply drag the application to the edge of your display, then release the application when you enter the next page.
* You can create an application folder by dragging an application over another application.
* Change the name of a folder: Click on the folder to open it, click on the name of the folder, and then type the name you want.
* You can remove apps from the folder by dragging the apps out of the folder.

Remove applications from Launchpad

* In Launchpad, long-click an application till all the applications start jiggling.

❖ Click on the application's Uninstall button ⊗ .

Apple ID

The account that gives you access to all Apple services is known as **Apple ID**. You can use your Apple ID to download applications from the Application Store; access media in Apple Books, Apple TV, & Apple Music, and more.

Note: If you forget your Apple ID login code, you do not have to create another Apple ID. Simply click the **"Forgot your Apple ID or password?"** button in the login window to recover your passcode.

All in one place: You can manage everything that's related to your Apple ID in one location. On your Mac, open Systems Setting—you'll see your Apple ID & Family Sharing settings at the upper part of the side bar. To login with Apple ID, if you have not, click the **Sign in with your Apple ID** button in the upper part of the side bar.

Manage family members, parental controls, purchases, and more.

Ashley Rico

Ashley Rico
ashley_rico1@icloud.com

Name, Phone, Email

Password & Security

Payment & Shipping

Update account information.

iCloud

Turn iCloud on or off.

Media & Purchases

Manage media accounts.

Family Sharing

Devices

Ashley's MacBook Pro
MacBook Pro

See all devices signed in with your Apple ID.

Update account, payment, & security details.
In Systems Settings, click on Apple ID in the side bar, then choose one of the items to review & update the details associated with your account.

❖ Overview.
❖ Name, Phone, Email.
❖ Password and security.
❖ Payments and Shipping.
❖ iCloud.
❖ Media and purchases.

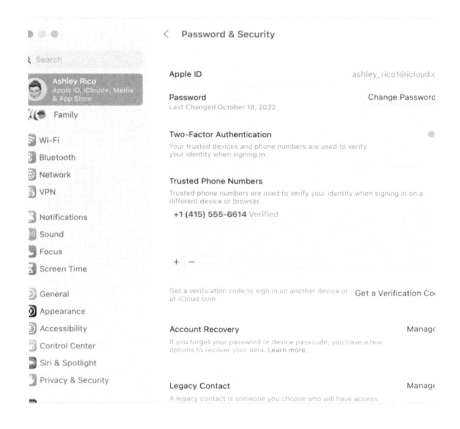

MacBook Air trackpad

You can do a lot with simple trackpad movements like scrolling through web pages, rotating images, zooming in or out on documents, etc. on your MacBook.

Click: Press anywhere on your Trackpad. Or activate the **Tap to Click** feature in Trackpad Settings and just tap the trackpad.

Force click: click the Trackpad & press deeper.

Secondary click (I.e. right click): click with two of your fingers to view the shortcut menu.

Two-finger scrolling: Swipe down or up with 2 of your fingers to scroll.

Zoom: Use your thumb and one of your fingers to pinch closed or open to zoom out or in on web pages & images.

Swipe to flip: Use 2 of your fingers to swipe to the right or left to flip through websites, docs, etc. —just like turning pages in a book.

Open Launchpad: pinch closed with 4 or 5 of your fingers to reveal the Launchpad, then click on an application in Launchpad to launch it.

Swipe between applications: Use 3 of your fingers to swipe to the right or left to switch from one full-screen application to another.

Personalize your gestures. In Systems Setting, click on Trackpad in the side bar. You can carry out any of the below:

- Get more info about every gesture

- Personalize other trackpad features
- Choose the click pressure you want
- Decide whether to use pressure-sensing features or not

BASIC SETTINGS

Shut down your device

❖ Select Apple menu , then click on Shut Down.

If you do not want the windows that are open before you shut down your device to reopen when you restart your device, unselect the **Reopen windows when logging back in** feature.

The MacBook shuts down completely when the screen goes black.

Note: Wait until your MacBook is completely shut down before you close it.

Note: You can force-shutdown your device if needed (for instance, if your MacBook is unresponsive) by long-pressing the power button till it shuts down. Unsaved changes in open documents may be lost.

Restart your MacBook

❖ Select Apple menu, then click on Restart.
   If you do not want the windows that are open to reopen when your device restarts, unselect the **Reopen windows when logging back in** feature.

Put your device to sleep or wake it

When you aren't making use of your MacBook, you can put it to sleep to save power.

Put your device to sleep

Carry out any of the below to put your Mac to sleep:

❖ Select Apple menu , then click on Sleep.
❖ Close your MacBook's display

Wake your device from sleep

Carry out any of the below to wake your device:

❖ Press one of the keys on your keyboard or click the trackpad or mouse.
❖ Open the display on your MacBook.

Connect your device to the Internet

Whether you are in your house, at work, or on the go, you can connect to the Internet with your MacBook. The 2 most common ways to access the Internet are making use of WiFi (wireless) or Ethernet (wired). If both of these are unavailable, you can use Instant Hotspot.

Use WiFi

If you are within range of a WiFi network, you can try to connect to it.

Join a public WiFi network

❖ Click on the WiFi icon 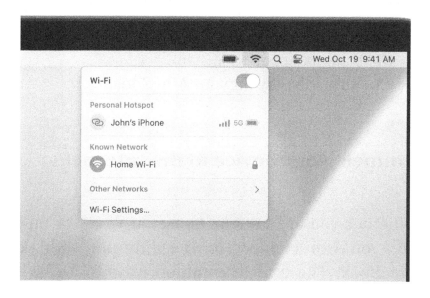 in the menu bar on your MacBook, then select the network you plan on joining.
If you can't find the network you plan to join, click on the **Other Networks** button to show nearby WiFi networks.

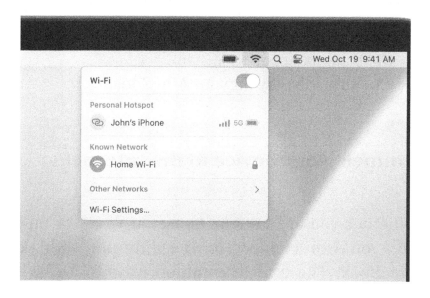

❖ If prompted, insert the network password and then click on **Join**.

Join a hidden Wi-Fi network

To join a hidden network, you need to know the name, security protocol & passcode of the private network.

❖ Click on the WiFi icon 🛜 in the menu bar on your MacBook, click on the **Other Networks** button, and then click on **Others** at the lower part of the Other Networks list.

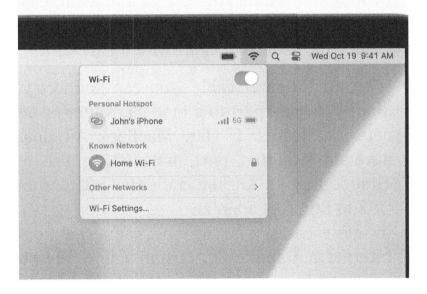

❖ Type the wireless network's name in the Network Name box.
❖ Click on the Security drop-down menu, then select the type of security the network is using.

❖ Fill in the info for any additional boxes that are shown, like the username & passcode, and then click on the **Join** button.

Connect with Ethernet

You can connect to the internet using Ethernet, either via an Ethernet network or via a cable modem or DSL. If you are making use of a modem, ensure the modem is switched on & connected to a wall jack using the cable that came with the modem.

❖ With an Ethernet cable, you can connect your Mac's Ethernet port to a modem, router or other network devices. If your MacBook Air doesn't have an Ethernet port, try making use of a Thunderbolt to Gigabit Ethernet adapter or a USB to Ethernet adapter.
In most cases, you will be connected to the Internet automatically. If not, follow the steps below to access network settings. If you're not sure what to enter, contact your network administrator or ISP.

❖ Select Apple menu > Systems Setting, then click on Network in the side bar. (You might have to scroll down.)

❖ Click on Ethernet Services on the right, and then click on **Advanced**.

❖ If you want, activate or deactivate the **Limit IP Address Tracking** feature.

❖ In the side bar, click on TCP/IP, click on the Configure IPv4 drop-down menu, and then select the configuration method recommended by your ISP.

   ➢ Manually: Pick this option if you received a custom IP address, router address & a subnet mask from your ISP, then insert those values.

   ➢ Use DHCP with manual address: Select this option if you were sent a specific IP address & your ISP makes use of DHCP, then insert the IP address.

   ➢ Use DHCP: Select this option if your ISP sent you an IP address automatically.

❖ If you have to enter search domain or DNS server settings, click on the **DNS** button in the side bar and then insert the info you were sent.

❖ If you have to enter WINS settings, click on the **WIN** button in the side bar and then insert the info you were sent.

❖ If you have to enter proxy server settings, click on the **Proxy** button in the side bar and then insert the info you were sent.

- ❖ If you have to setup Ethernet hardware settings, click on the **Hardware** button in the side bar and then insert the info you were sent.
- ❖ Click on OK.

Use an iPad or iPhone to connect your MacBook to the internet

Your MacBook can use your iPhone or iPad's Personal Hotspot (cellular version) to connect to the Internet.

Before trying to connect, ensure Personal Hotspot is activated on your iPad or iPhone (enter the Settings application> Personal Hotspot on your device).

Use Wi-Fi to connect

- ❖ Ensure that your MacBook & your iPhone or iPad are using the same Apple ID.
- ❖ Click on the WiFi status icon 🛜 in the menu bar on your MacBook, then select your iPad or iPhone.
  After connecting to the personal hotspot, you can use the WiFi menu to check the cellular signal strength.

When you aren't making use of the hotspot, your device will automatically disconnect to save battery life.

Connect via USB

❖ Use the USB cable that came with your device to connect your iPad or iPhone to your MacBook.
❖ If a **"Trust This Computer?"** alert is displayed on your iPad or iPhone screen, simply touch the **Trust** button.

Check the USB connection status & configure options

❖ Select Apple menu 🍎 > Systems Setting, then click on Network 🌐 in the sidebar. (You might have to scroll down.)
❖ Click on [your device USB] on the right, then click on the **Details** button.
❖ If you want, carry out any of the below:
  ➢ Activate the **Disable Unless Needed** feature
  ➢ Activate Low Data Mode
❖ Tap OK

View & edit files with Quick Look

The **Quick Look** feature provides a quick and full-size preview of almost any file type without opening the file. You can rotate images, cut video & audio, and use Markup - in the Quick Look window.

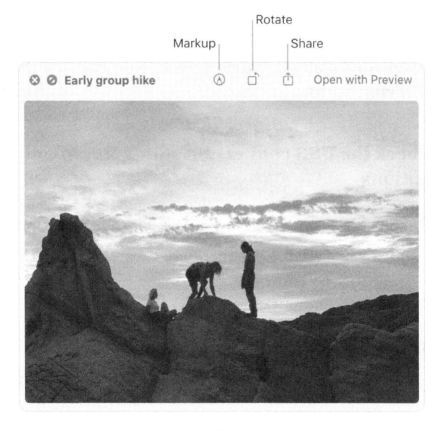

Tip: You can use the Quick Look feature for items on your desktop, in Finder windows, in messages & e-mails, and elsewhere.

❖ Select an item, then press the Space bar.
The Quick Look window will open. If you select multiple items, the last item you selected will be displayed first.

❖ In the Quick Look window, carry out any of the below:

➢ Change the size of the window: Drag the window's corners. Or click on the Full-Screen icon on the upper-left edge of the window. To leave the full screen, click the Exit Full-Screen icon in the lower part of the window.

➢ Zoom out & in of an item: Press Cmd-(+) to zoom in or Cmd-(-) to zoom out.

➢ Markup an item: Click on the Annotate icon

➢ Trim a video or audio clip: Click on the Cut icon , and then drag the yellow handle to the cut bar. Click on the Play button to test the changes you've made. Click the **Revert** button to start over. When you are done, click on the **Done** button, then choose to replace the original file or create another one.

➢ Display items in the grid view (if you've selected more than one item): Click on the Grid icon⊡ or press Cmd-Return.

➢ Share an item: Click on the Share icon⬆, then select one of the sharing options

➢ Copy an item's subject: If the item is a picture, you can isolate the subject from the photo's background. Ctrl-click the picture, then select the **Copy Subject** option. You can now paste the subject in an e-mail, note, text message, or document.

❖ When you are done, press the Space bar or click on the Close icon⊗ to close the Quick Look window.

Take a screenshot or record your Mac's screen

You can snap a picture (called a screenshot) or record your Mac's screen by making use of Screenshot or keyboard shortcuts. **Screenshot** provides a toolbar that lets you easily capture pictures of your screen and it also allows you to record your Mac's screen, with options to control what you're capturing

Take a photo or screen recording using Screenshot

❖ Press Shift-Cmd-5 (or use Launchpad) to launch Screenshot & show the tools.

❖ Click on one of the tools to select what you want to record or snap.
   For a part of your display, drag the frame to change its position or drag the edges to resize the area you would like to record or snap.

➤ Click on this icon to snap the whole display

➤ Click on the Window icon to snap a window

➤ Click on the Segment icon to snap a portion of your display

➤ Click on the Record Screen icon to record the whole display

➤ Click on the Record Segment icon to record a portion of your Mac's display.

❖ If desired, click on **Options**.
The available options vary depending on whether you are capturing a screenshot or recording the screen. For example, you can specify where to save the file or choose to display the mouse cursor or clicks.

❖ Start taking the screenshot or recording your screen:

➤ For the full screen or part of it: Click on the **Capture** button.

➤ For a window: Hover the cursor, then click on the window.

➤ For recordings: Click on the **Record** button. To stop recording, click on the Stop icon ⬤ on the menu bar.

When the Display Floating Thumbnail option is enabled, you can carry out any of the below while the thumbnail is temporarily displayed in the lower-right corner of your display:

❖ Swipe to the right to store the file immediately.
❖ Drag the thumbnail into an e-mail, a note, a Finder window or a document.

Use keyboard shortcuts to capture screenshots

You can use different keyboard shortcuts on your MacBook to capture screenshots. The file is stored on the desktop.

❖ Press Shift-Cmd-3 to snap the whole display
❖ To snap a part of your display, simply press Shift-Cmd-4, then hover the cursor to where you want to begin the screenshot. Press the trackpad or mouse button, drag over the section you plan to snap, and then release the trackpad or mouse button.

- ❖ To snap a window or the menu bar, simply press Shift-Cmd-4, and then press the Space bar. Hover the cursor over the menu bar or the window to select it, then click
- ❖ Press Shift-Cmd-5 to launch Screenshot
- ❖ Press Shift-Cmd-6 to snap the

You can personalize these shortcuts in the keyboard settings. Select Apple menu > Systems Setting, click on Keyboard in the side bar, click on Keyboards Shortcuts on the right, and then click on the **Screenshots** option. (You might have to scroll down.)

Screenshots are stored as png files & screen recordings are stored as MOV files. The file name begins with "Screen Recording" or "Screenshot" and includes the time & date.

Change the brightness of your Mac screen

You can change your device screen brightness manually or automatically.

Use the brightness key

On your MacBook's keyboard, press the brightness up button ☼ or the brightness down button ☼ .

Adjust the brightness automatically

❖ Select Apple menu > Systems Setting, then click on Displays 🔅 on the side bar. (You might have to scroll down.)
❖ Activate the **"Automatically adjust brightness"** feature on the right side of the window.

Adjust the brightness manually

❖ Select Apple menu > Systems Setting, then click on the Displays button on the side bar. (You might have to scroll down.)

❖ Move the Brightness slider on the right to change your MacBook's screen brightness.

Increase or decrease your MacBook's volume

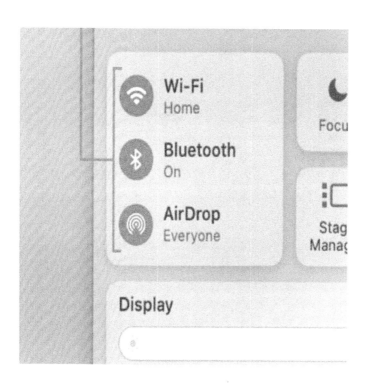

To increase or decrease your Mac's volume, click on the Sound Control in the Controls Centre or menu bar, then slide the slider to change the volume level.

If you can't find the Sound Control in the menu bar, select Apple menu 🍎 > Systems Setting, then click on the **Controls Centre** button 🎛 on the side bar. (You might add to scroll down.) Click on the drop-down menu beside Sound on the right, then select one of the options.

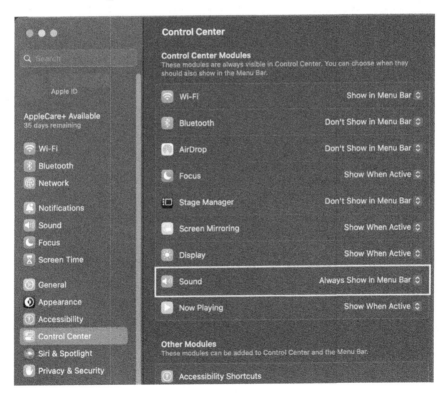

Launch applications on your device

You can have more than one application open at the same time on your device. The fastest way to launch an application on your device is to click on the icon of the application in the Dock.

If you can't find the app's icon in the Dock, there are other ways to launch the application on your device:

❖ Click on the Launchpad icon in the Dock, and then click on the app's icon.

❖ You can use Siri to launch apps. You could say "open the mail app"

❖ Click on the Spotlight button $\mathcal{Q}$ on the menu bar, type the name of the application in the search box, and then press the Return key.

❖ If you've recently made use of an application, Select Apple menu > Recent Items, then select the application.

❖ In the Dock, click on the Finder icon , click on the **Applications** button in the Finder window's sidebar, and then double-click the application.

Manage application windows on your MacBook

When you launch an application or the Finder on your MacBook, a window will open on the desktop. Only one application will be active at a time; the application name (in bold) & the application menus will be displayed in the menu bar.

Some applications, like Mail or Safari, allow you to open multiple windows or different types of windows simultaneously. There are many ways to manage open application windows on your device.

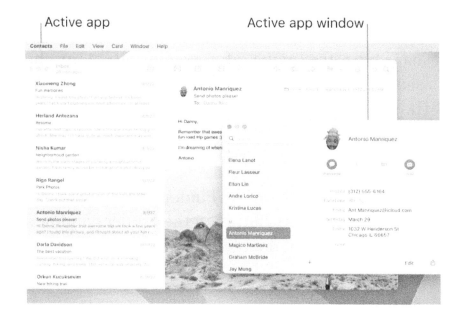

Active app   Active app window

Move, align, & merge application windows

Carry out any of the below on your MacBook:

❖ You can move a window by dragging the window by its title bar to the desired position on your screen.

❖ Move a window to one side of your display: Long-press the Option button while moving the cursor over the green icon in the upper left edge of the window, then select the **Move Window to the Right Side of the Display** or the **Move Window to the Left Side of the Display** option from the menu that pops-up. The window will fill one side of your display; the Dock & menu bar will still be visible.

To take the window back to its original size & position, hold down the Option key, hover the cursor over the green icon 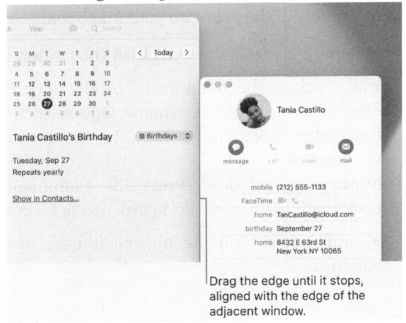, then select the **Revert** button.

❖ Align windows: Drag one window near another window—as the window gets close to the other one, it will align without overlapping. You can place multiple windows adjacent to each other.

You can make adjacent windows the same size by dragging the edge you plan on resizing—as it gets close to the adjacent window's edge, it will align with the edge & stop.

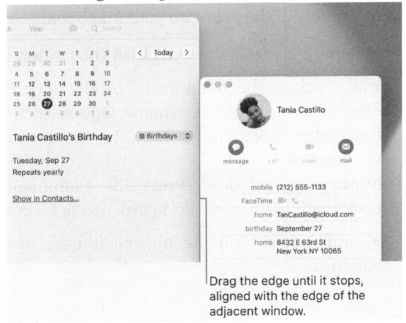

Drag the edge until it stops, aligned with the edge of the adjacent window.

❖ Merge an application's windows into a single tabbed window: In an application, select Window, then select the **Merge All Windows** option. If an application has more than one window view (for example, the Mail application with a new message window & the viewer window), just the active view will be merged.

To make one of the tabs a different window again, select the tab, select Window, then select the **Move Tab to New Window** option, or you can simply drag the tab out of the window.

Minimize or maximize application windows

Carry out any of the below on your MacBook:

❖ Maximize a window: Hold down the Option key while clicking the green icon on the upper-left edge of the application window. Option-click the icon once more to go back to the previous window size.

❖ Minimize a window: Press the Command-M combination on your keyboard or click on the Minimize icon on the upper-left edge of the window.

You can manually change the size of most windows. Drag the edge of the window (side, bottom, or top) or double-click one of the edges to expand the window's size.

Quickly switch between application windows

Carry out any of the below on your MacBook:

❖ Go to the previous application: Press the Command-Tab combination on your keyboard.
❖ Navigate through all open applications: Hold down the Command button, press the Tab button, then press the Right or Left arrow till you reach the desired application. Release the Command button.
If you change your mind while scrolling through the applications & you do not want to change applications any longer, press the Esc button & release the Command button.

Close one or all windows for an application

Carry out any of the below on your MacBook:

❖ You can close a window by clicking the Close icon on the upper-left edge of the window or by pressing Command-W.

❖ Press the Option-Command-W combination to close all open windows for an application.
❖ Press Command-Q to close/quit an application

Use applications in full screen

A lot of applications on your device are compatible with the full-screen mode—an application that fills the whole display—so you can use every inch of the display and work without the distraction of your desktop.

❖ Hover the cursor to the green icon in the upper-left edge of the window, then select the **Enter Full Screen** option from the pop-up menu, or click on the icon .

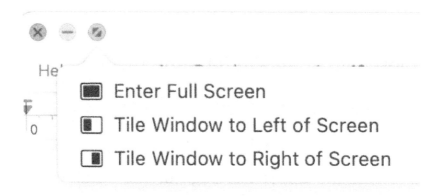

❖ You can carry out any of the below in full screen:
  ➢ Hide or display the menu bar: Hover the cursor away or to the top of your display. If you have disabled the option to hide & display the menu bar in full screen, the menu bar is always displayed.
  ➢ Hide or display the Dock: Hover the cursor to or away from the location of the Dock.
  ➢ Move from one application in full screen to another: Use 3 or 4 of your fingers to swipe to the right or left on the trackpad.
❖ To exit Full Screen, hover the cursor over the green button once more, then select the **Exit Full-Screen** option from the pop-up menu or click on the icon .

Use applications in Split View

A lot of applications on your device are compatible with the Split View feature, which allows you to work in 2 applications side by side simultaneously.

❖ Hover the cursor over the green icon in the upper-left edge of the window, then select the **Tile Window on the Right Side of the Screen** or the **Tile Window to the Left Side of the Screen** option from the pop-up menu.

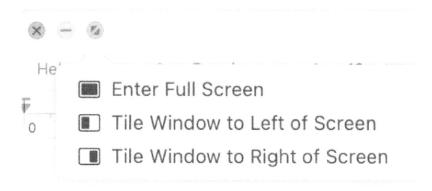

❖ On the other side of your display, click on the 2nd application you want to use.
The Split View will be created in the new desktop space.

❖ Carry out any of the below in Split View:

> Hide or display the menu bar: Hover the cursor away or to the top of your display. If you have disabled the option to hide & display the menu bar in full screen, the menu bar is always displayed.

> Hide or display the Dock: Hover the cursor to or away from the location of the Dock.

> Display or hide the title & toolbar of a window: Click on the window, then hover the cursor away or to the top of your display.

> Switch sides: Use the title & tool bar of a window to drag the window to the other side of the Split View.

> Make one of the windows bigger: Hover the cursor over the separator bar that can be found in the center of the Split view and drag it to the right or left. Double-click the separator bar to go back to the original size.

➤ Use another application on one side: Click on the application window, hover the cursor over the green icon in the upper-left edge, select the **Replace Tiled Window** option, and then click on the window you would like to use. If you decide not to change the window at this point, click on the desktop to return to it.

➤ Move an application window to your Mac desktop: Click on the application window, hover the cursor over the green button in the upper-left edge of the window, and then select the Move Window to Desktop option. The application will be displayed on the desktop.

The other application will switch to full screen in its own space; to go back to the application, press the Control-Up Arrow keyboard combination or simply use 3 or 4 of your fingers to swipe up to open **Mission Control**, then click on the application in the Space bar.

➢ Use one of the windows in full screen: Click on the application window, hover the cursor over the green icon in the upper left edge of the window, then select the **Make Window Full-Screen** option.

The other application will switch to full screen in its own space; to go back to the application, press the Control-Up Arrow keyboard combination or simply use 3 or 4 of your fingers to swipe up to open **Mission Control**, then click on the application in the Space bar.

Personalize the desktop photo

You can change the image displayed on your desktop. Select from a variety of images or colours provided by Apple, or use one of yours.

❖ Select Apple menu, click on Systems Setting, then click on the Wallpaper button on the side bar. (You might have to scroll down.)

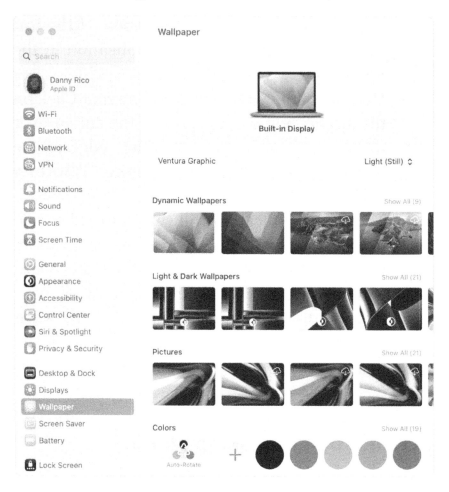

❖ Choose an image from one of the following categories:

- Dynamic wallpapers: These images change gradually throughout the day based on your location. If you activate the Location Service feature (in the privacy and security settings), the image will change according to the time zone displayed in the Time and Date settings.
- Light and Dark Wallpapers: These images change from light to dark at sunset depending on your location. However, if you select Dark Mode in the Appearance setting or when setting up your device, the desktop image will be a dark still picture. To stop making use of a dark still picture, click on the drop-down menu, then select Auto or Light.
- Pictures.
- Colour: Use a very colourful background for your desktop. Click on the Add icon + to pick a colour not shown.
- Add Folder / Add Photo Album: Select this option to use one of the pictures in your photo album or from a folder. To add a folder, click on the Add Folder button and then select one of the folders. To add a photo album, click on the **Add Photo Album** button, then select Albums (all albums) or a specific album.

  If your pictures look blurry, try making use of a larger image, like a 1024 by 768-pixel image.

❖ Carry out any of the below to edit a custom desktop colour or photo:

➢ Rotate through multiple images or colours on the desktop: Click on the **Auto-Rotate** button beside a specific folder or colour to periodically change the images or colours on the desktop. Use the controls at the top of Wallpaper settings to adjust the timing or you can select random rotation.

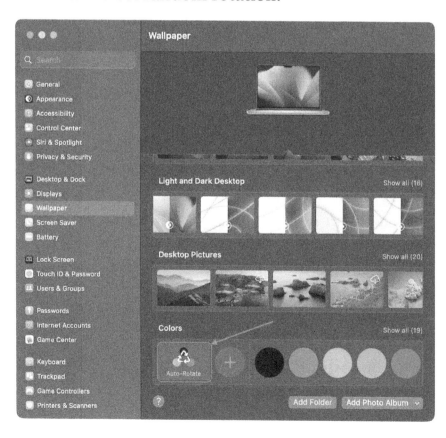

> Change the layout or size of your desktop wallpaper: Select one of the options from the drop-down menu at the top of Wallpaper Settings.

Tip: To quickly use an existing picture in the Photos application, launch the Photos application, select the picture, click on the Share icon 📤 in the tool bar, and then select the **Set Wallpaper** option.

You can also use any photo you find on the internet as your desktop wallpaper. Ctrl-click on the picture in the browser, and choose the **Use Image as Desktop Photo** option.

Use light or dark mode on your Mac

Light   Dark   Auto

You can use a dark or light theme for windows, the Dock, menu bar, & inbuilt applications on your device, or have it automatically adjust from light to dark.

* Select Apple menu, click on Systems Setting, then click on the Appearance button in the side bar. (You might have to scroll down.)
* On the right, choose Auto, Dark, or Light.
    ➤ Dark or Dark Mode darkens the colour scheme, so the content you are working on will stand out.
    Tip: You can quickly activate or deactivate Dark Mode in the Controls Centre. In the menu bar, click on Control Center, click on the **Display** button, and then click on Dark Mode.
    ➤ Auto changes the Appearance based on your Night Shift schedule

Change Night Shift settings

Use Night Shift to shift your Mac's screen to the warmer side of the colour spectrum. Warmer display colours are more pleasant to the eyes when using your device at night or in low-light conditions.

To adjust these settings, Select Apple menu, click on Systems Setting, click on the Displays button in the side bar (You might have to scroll down), and then click on the Night Shift button on the right side of the window.

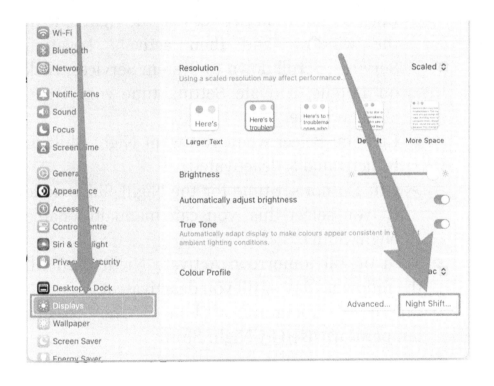

❖ Schedule: Select one of the options to automatically activate Night Shift at specified times.

➢ Sunset to Sunrise: Activate the Night Shift mode from sunset to sunrise.
You have to activate Location Services before this option can function. Select Apple menu, click on System Settings, and then click on the Privacy & Security ⬚ button in the sidebar. Click on Location Services on the right side of the window, and then activate Location Services. Scroll down to System Services, click on Details, activate Setting time zone, then click on Done.
➢ Custom: Select when you want Night Shift to be activated & deactivated.
➢ Off: Do not set time for the Night Shift mode (if you select this, you can manually enable Night Shift).
❖ Turn on till tomorrow: Activate Night Shift till the following day or till you deactivate it.
❖ Colour temperature: Change the colour temperature used by Night Shift.

Use a screen saver

A screen saver can help to hide the desktop when you are away from your MacBook or if you need more privacy.

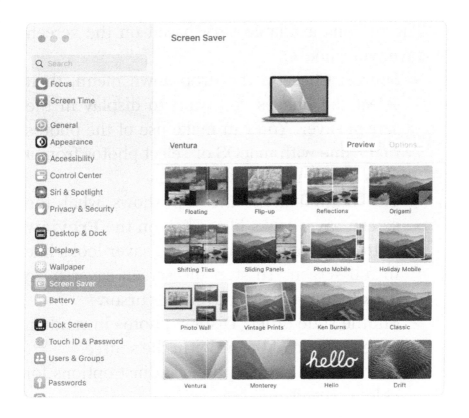

Personalize the screen saver on your MacBook

❖ Select Apple menu > Systems Setting, then click on the Screen Saver button on the sidebar. (You might have to scroll down.)
❖ Click on one of the screen-saver thumbnails on the right side of the window, then make changes to the settings.

The options available vary based on the screen saver you choose.

> Source: Click on the drop-down menu, then select the images you want to display in the screen saver. You can make use of the photos that came with macOS or select photos from a folder or your Photos Library.

The thumbnail at the top shows what the screen saver looks like. Click on the **Preview** button to see what the screen saver looks like in full screen. To stop the screen saver & go back to the settings, hover the cursor.

> Shuffle slide order: Display photos in random order instead of the order in the source.

> More screen saver options: Adjust options for colour, speed, etc.

❖ Click on OK.

To display the time in the screen saver, activate the **Show with clock** feature.

Start or stop the screen saver on your device

❖ The screen saver will automatically start anytime your MacBook remains idle for the amount of time you set in Screensaver preferences.

To make changes to how long your MacBook can be idle before the screensaver comes up, select

Apple menu⌘ > Systems Setting, then click on the Lock Screen🔒 button on the sidebar (You might have to scroll down.), and then select settings on the right side of the window.

❖ Press any of the keys, tap the trackpad, or move the mouse to stop the screen saver & display the desktop.

Require a password when you wake your MacBook

To keep data safe when you're away from your MacBook, set it to require a passcode when you wake it from sleep.

❖ Select Apple menu⌘ > Systems Setting, then click on the Lock Screen🔒 button on the sidebar. (You might have to scroll down.)

❖ Click on the drop-down menu beside "Require a password when the screensaver begins or turns off," then select the amount of time that elapses before the password is prompted.

Change a user's login photo

You can change the image that appears beside your username or other usernames in the login window on your MacBook. You can select one of the photos from your photos library, use your Mac's camera to snap a new picture, select an emoji or Memoji, etc. Your user login photo is also displayed as your Apple ID photo & My Card in the Contacts application.

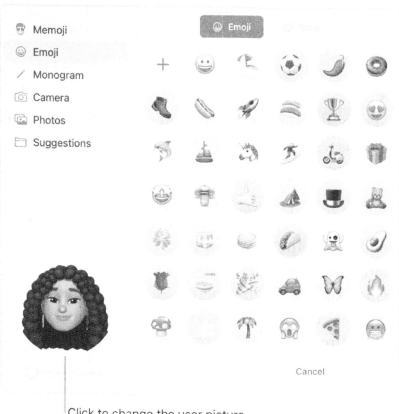

Click to change the user picture.

❖ Select Apple menu 🍎 > Systems Setting, then click on the Users and Group 👥 button on the sidebar. (You might have to scroll down.)
❖ Click on the user picture on the right side of the window, then carry out any of the below:
➢ Choose one of the Memojis: Click on Memoji, then click on the Add icon ✚ to choose & create a facial picture. Or pick any of the displayed Memoji, and then choose one of the styles & poses.

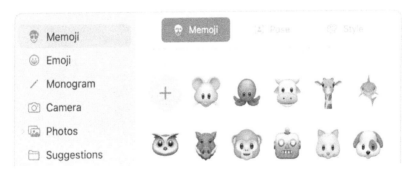

➢ Select one of the emojis: Click on the **Emoji** button, then click on the Add icon ✚ to choose one of the images from the emoji library. Or choose any of the emojis shown and choose a style.

> Choose a Monogram: Click on the **Monogram** button, choose one of the background colors and then type your initials.

> Choose one of the pictures from your Photo library: Click on the **Photos** button. To view pictures from an album, click on the arrow ⟩ beside Photos in the side bar, click on the album you want, and then choose one of the pictures.

> Use your Mac camera to snap a photo: Click on the **Camera** button. Frame your shot and

click on the Capture icon. You can retake the
picture as much as you want.

➢ Choose a recommended photo: Click on the
Suggestions button, and then choose one of
the pictures.

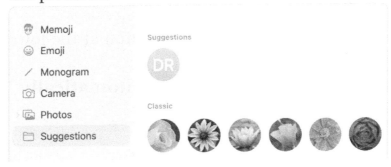

❖ After selecting a photo, you can adjust its appearance. Carry out any of the below:
  ➢ Change the picture position: Drag the image around within the circle.
  ➢ Zoom out or in: Move the slider to the right or left.
❖ Click on the Save button.

Set your MacBook to log out when you are not using it

You can configure your MacBook to automatically log off the current user account after not being used for a period of time. This will help keep your data safe when your MacBook is unattended.

❖ Select Apple menu, click on System Settings, then click on the Privacy & Security button in the sidebar.
❖ Click on the **Advanced** button at the lower part of the window
❖ Activate the **Log out automatically after inactivity** feature.

❖ Click on the **Log Out after** drop-down menu, then select how long before the user is logged out.

Change your Mac's login password

To protect your privacy, it is important to change your login passcode periodically.

Note: Your login passcode is the passcode you insert to unlock your MacBook when you switch it on or wake it.

❖ Select Apple menu > Systems Setting, then click on the Users and Group button in the side bar. (You might have to scroll down.)

❖ Click on the Info icon ⓘ beside your username on the right part of the window.

❖ Click on the **Change password** button.

❖ Type your passcode in the Old password box.

❖ Type the new passcode in the New Password box, and then type it once more in the Verify box.

Click on the Secure icon �🔑 beside the New Password box to help you choose a strong password.

❖ Type a hint that can help you to remember the passcode.

The hint will appear after you type the wrong passcode 3 times in a row or if you click on the question mark in the passcode box in the login window.

❖ Click on the **Change Password** button.

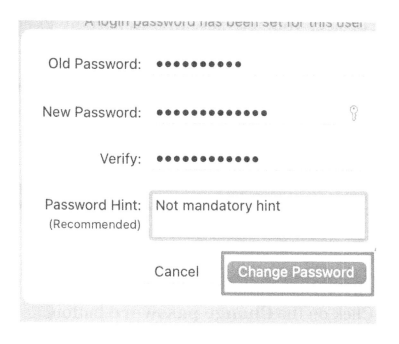

Reset your MacBook login passcode using your Apple ID

Sometimes you need to reset your login passcode, for instance, if you forgot your login password and you cannot use the passcode hint to remember the passcode.

If you don't see a question mark, shut down your Mac, then restart.

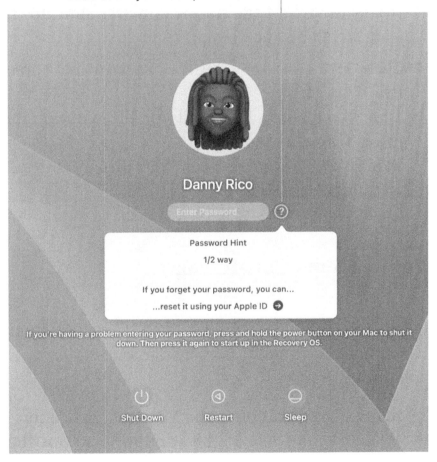

If you've associated your users account with your Apple ID, you can reset the login passcode using your Apple ID.

❖ Click on the question mark 🔘 beside the password box.
  If you can't find the question mark, shut down your MacBook, then restart it.
❖ Click on the arrow 🔘 beside "Reset using Apple ID."
❖ Type your Apple ID details in the appropriate fields, then click on Next
  Adhere to the directives on your display to reset your login passcode.

Create Memoji in Messages

Create a custom Memoji that matches your personality and send it in your messages to express your mood.

❖ Select a conversation in the Message application.
❖ At the bottom left of the window, click on the Apps icon 🔘, and then click on the Memoji Stickers icon 🔘.

❖ Click on the Add icon ✛ (for your 1ˢᵗ Memoji) or the More icon ••• , then adhere to the directives on your display to create & personalize your Memoji.

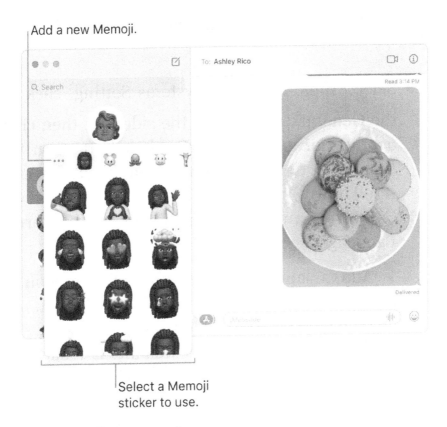

Add a new Memoji.

Select a Memoji sticker to use.

❖ Click on the **Done** button.

Change the language your MacBook uses

You can use different languages for each application. For instance, if your system language is set to Simple Chinese, but you would like to use English for a certain application, you can.

Change the system language

❖ Select Apple menu > Systems Setting, click on the General button in the side bar, then click on the **Language and Region** button on the right side of the window. (You might have to scroll down.)

❖ Carry out any of the below in the Preferred Languages section:

  ➢ Add a language: Click on the Add icon , choose 1 or more languages from the list, and then click on the **Add** button.

  ➢ You can change the default language by dragging a language to the beginning of the language list.

  Note: You may have to restart your device for all changes to take effect.

Choose the language for each application

❖ Select Apple menu > Systems Setting, click on the General button in the side bar, then click on the **Language and Region** button on the right side of the window. (You might have to scroll down.)

❖ Head over to Applications, then carry out any of the below:

➢ Select a language for an application: Click on the Add icon , select an application & language from the drop-down menu, and then click on the **Add** button.

➢ Change the language for a listed app: Select the application and choose another language from the drop-down menu.

➢ Remove an application from the list: Select the application, then click on the Remove icon . The application will use the default language from now on.

If the application is open, you may have to close & reopen it for the changes to take effect.

Make everything on your display bigger

You can change the resolution of your display to make everything on your Mac's screen appear bigger.

❖ Select Apple menu > Systems Setting, click on the Display button in the side bar. (You might have to scroll down.)
❖ Choose one of the resolutions on the right side of the window.
A lower resolution makes the size of everything on your display bigger.

Change text size

You can change the text size on your device.

❖ In applications: You can press Cmd-Plus (+) or Cmd-Minus (-) to change the text size when reading an email, message, article & webpage in applications, like Mail, Messages, News, & Safari.
❖ In desktop labels: Ctrl-click the desktop, select Show View Options

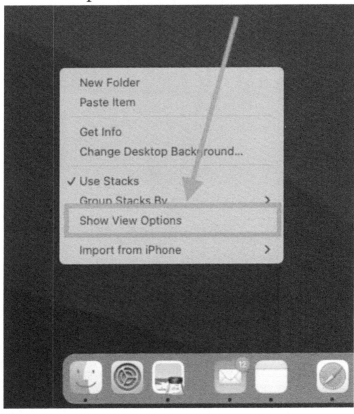

Click on the **Text Size** button in the menu that appears, and then select a text size.

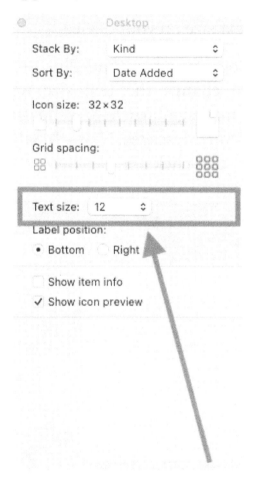

❖ In sidebars: Select Apple menu > Systems Setting, and click on the Appearance button in the side bar (You might have to scroll down.). Click on the drop-down menu beside "sidebar icon size" on the right side of the window, and then select one of the options.

❖ In File & Folder Names in the Finder: Select View > Show View Options. Click on the Text size drop-down menu, and then select one of the text sizes.

Change the size of icons

❖ On the desktop: Ctrl-click the desktop, select Show View Options, then slide the "Icon size" to the left or right.

❖ In sidebars: Select Apple menu > Systems Setting, and click on the Appearance button in the side bar (You might have to scroll down.). Click on the drop-down menu beside "sidebar icon size" on the right side of the window, and then select one of the options.
❖ In Finder windows: Select View > Show View Options. In List view & Icons view, select one of the icon sizes. In Gallery view, you can select one of the thumbnail sizes.

Control camera access on Mac

Some installed applications can use your Mac's camera to take pictures & videos. You can decide which applications are allowed to use your Mac's camera.

❖ Select Apple menu > Systems Setting, click on the Privacy and Security button in the side bar (You might have to scroll down.).
❖ Click on Camera
❖ Enable or disable access to the camera for each application in the list.

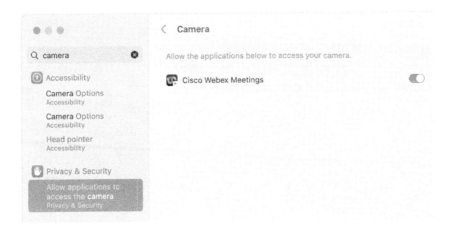

The list displays the applications you have installed that have asked to use the camera. If you disable access to an application, the next time the application tries to use the camera, you'll be prompted to turn it back on.

Note: The camera activates automatically when you launch an application that can use the camera. A green light next to the camera indicates that the camera is active.

Use the desktop stacks

Desktop stack on your MacBook organizes files on your desktop into different groups. After you save a file to your desktop, it is automatically added to the suitable stack.

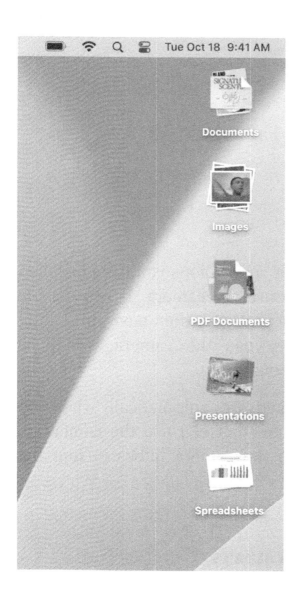

Activate desktop stacks

Click the desktop on your MacBook, then select View > Use Stacks or press the Ctrl-Cmd-0 keyboard combination. You can also Ctrl-click on the desktop and then select Use Stacks.

View the files in a stack

Swipe right or left on the stack using 2 fingers on the trackpad.

Expand or collapse a desktop stack

❖ Expand a stack: Click on the stack. After expanding the stack, double-click an item to open it.

❖ Click on the stack's Down Arrow icon to collapse the stack

Change the grouping of stacks on the desktop

You can group stacks by type (like PDF or pictures), date (like when the file was created or last opened), or Finder tag.

❖ Click the desktop on your MacBook, select View > Group Stacks By, then select one of the options. Or Ctrl-click on the desktop, select Group Stacks By, then select one of the options.

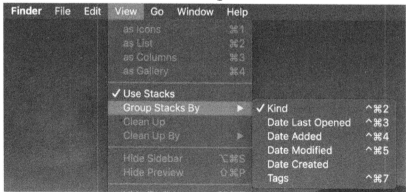

Uninstall applications

❖ Click the Finder button ▨ in the Dock, then click on Applications in the Finder window side bar.
❖ Carry out any of the below:
  ➢ If the application is in a folder: Open the application's folder to see if there's an Uninstaller. If you see [App] Uninstaller or Uninstall [Apps], double-click it, and then adhere to the directives on your display.
  ➢ If the application is not in the folder or does not have an Uninstaller: Drag the application from the Apps folder to the Trash (on the right edge of the Dock).

Use Hot Corners

Use the corners of your display as hot corners to start a quick action when you hover the cursor to one of the corners of your display. For instance, you can hover the cursor to the upper right corner of your display to lock your screen or hover the cursor to the lower right corner of your display to open a Quick Note.

❖ Select Apple menu, and click on Systems Settings

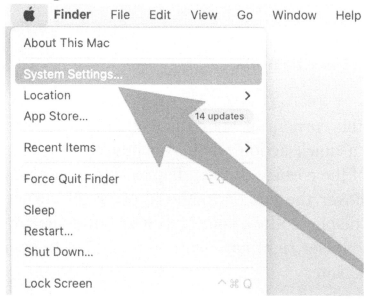

❖ Click on the Desktop and Dock 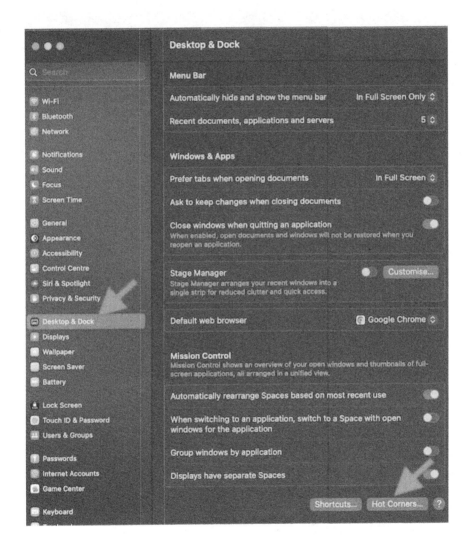 button on the sidebar, (Scroll, if necessary), then click on Hot Corners on the right side of your display.

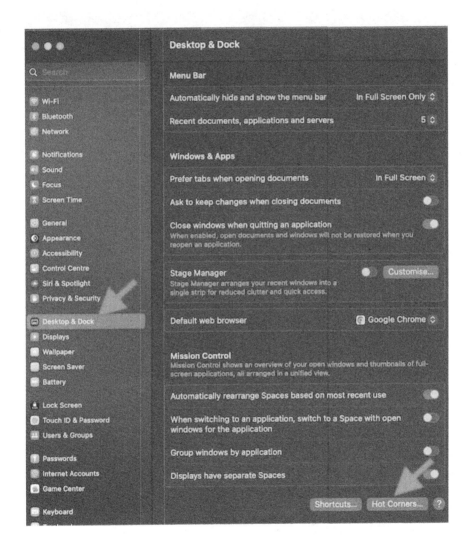

❖ Click on the drop-down menu for each corner you want to use, select one of the options from the menu, and then click on Done.

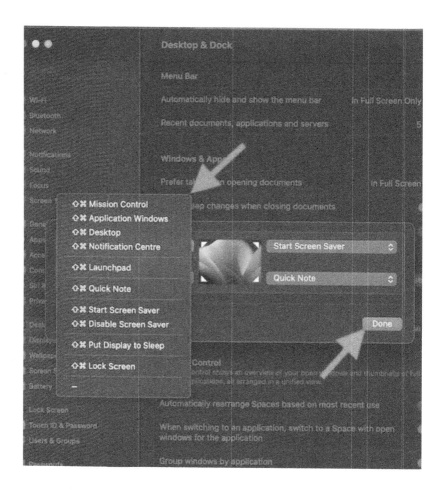

Use Live Text to interact with text in pictures

Use the Live Text feature to interact with text found in pictures in the Preview application. For instance, you can copy the text in a picture & paste it in an e-mail or note. You can check the meaning of a word; translate text into other languages, and more. If there's an e-mail address, site, or phone number in the picture, you can use it to open a webpage, make a call, or send an e-mail.

❖ In the Preview application , open a picture that has text in it.
❖ Position your cursor over the text, then drag to highlight the text
❖ Carry out any of the below:
  ➢ Copy the highlighted text: Ctrl-click on the selected text & select Copy (or press the Cmd-C combination). You can paste the text into another application.
  ➢ Check the definition of the text: Ctrl-click on the selected text & select Lookup[text]
  ➢ Translate text: Ctrl-click on the selected text, select Translate[text] and select one of the languages.
  ➢ Search for text online: Ctrl-click on the selected text & select Search With[Internet search engine].
  ➢ Share the text: Ctrl-click on the selected text, click on the **Share** button, and then select one of the sharing options.
  ➢ Call a number: Ctrl-click on the selected text, or click on the Down Arrow ∨, then select one of the options on your display.
  ➢ Contact an e-mail address: Ctrl-click on the selected text, or click on the Down Arrow ∨, then select one of the options on your display.

➤ Visit a site: Ctrl-click on the selected text, or click on the Down Arrow ⌄ , then select one of the options on your display.

Start a Quick Note

If you are working in another application & would like to quickly jot something down, you can start a Quick Note. The Quick Note will remain on your display while it is open so that you can add more info. Carry out any of the below to start a Quick Note:

❖ On your keyboard, long-press the Fn button or Globe button ⊕ , then press Q
❖ Use a hot corner: Hover the cursor to the lower-right corner of your display, then click on the note that pops-up.

Click on the Close icon ⊗ in the upper left edge of the Quick Note to close it.

STAGE MANAGER

Stage Manager allows MacBook users to multitask & get things done with ease. Change the windows' size to get the look you want, view multiple overlapping windows at the same time, etc.

The Stage Manager feature allows you can keep the application you are using in the middle of the desktop, while your recently used applications are neatly arranged on the left side of your display for easy access

Arrange, overlap, & resize windows in the optimal order. You can also arrange multiple applications on

your display to work together as a group in Stage Manager. After switching to a group, all the applications in the group will open in the middle of your display.

Enable or disable Stage Manager

You can quickly switch between the Stage Manager & normal windows to use the method that works best for what you want to do.

Carry out any of the below on your Mac:

❖ Select Apple menu > Systems Setting, then click on the **Desktop and Dock** button in the side bar. (You might have to scroll down.) Head over to Window & App on the right, then activate or deactivate the **Stage Manager** feature.

❖ Click on Controls Centre in the menu bar, then click on Stage Manager to activate or deactivate it.

Use Stage Manager

Carry out any of the below on your Mac:

❖ Switch applications: Click on one of the applications on the left side of your display.

❖ Arrange windows: Arrange, overlap, & change the size of windows to suit your tasks.
❖ Group applications: Drag an application from the left side of your display to add the application to a group of applications in the middle of your display.
❖ Ungroup applications: Drag an application to the left side of your display to remove it from the group

If you've disabled "Recent Apps" in the Stage Manager settings, the list of applications on the left is hidden. Hover your cursor to the left edge of your display to reveal them.

Display or hide Stage Manager in the menu bar

You can choose to display Stage Manager in the menu bar.

❖ Select Apple menu > Systems Setting, then click on the **Controls Center** button in the side bar. (You might have to scroll down.)
❖ Click on the drop-down menu beside Stage Manager on the right and then select the **Show**

in Menu Bar option or the **Don't Show in Menu Bar** option.

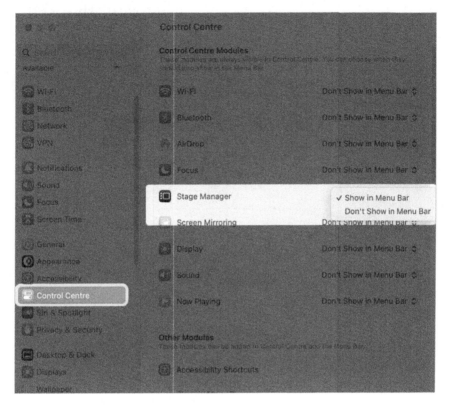

Change Stage Manager settings

❖ Select Apple menu > Systems Setting, then click on the **Desktop and Dock** button in the side bar. (You might have to scroll down.)

❖ Head over to Window & App on the right, click on the **Customize** button beside Stage Manager, and then activate or deactivate the settings below:

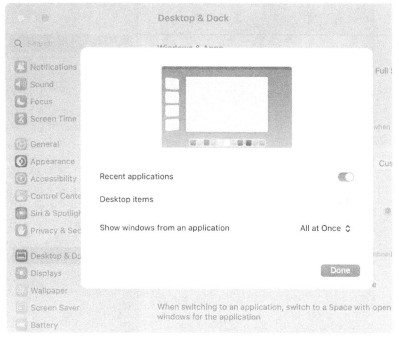

➢ Recent apps: Display recently used applications on the left side of the display.
If you disable this option, recently used applications will be hidden - Hover your cursor to the left edge of your display to reveal them.

➢ Desktop Items: Display items on your desktop.

If you disable this option, desktop items will be hidden - click on the desktop to display them whenever you want to access them.

❖ Click on the "Show windows from application" menu, then select any of the options:

➢ One at a Time: Display only the last used window for an application when you switch the application.
To switch to another window when this option is disabled, click on the application on the left once more to open the next window.

➢ All at Once: Display every available window for an application when you switch to the application.

❖ Click on the **Done** button

TOUCH ID

You can use your registered fingerprint to unlock your device, sign into 3rd party applications, authenticate purchases from the iTunes Store, Apps Store, etc. & make online purchases with Apple Pay.

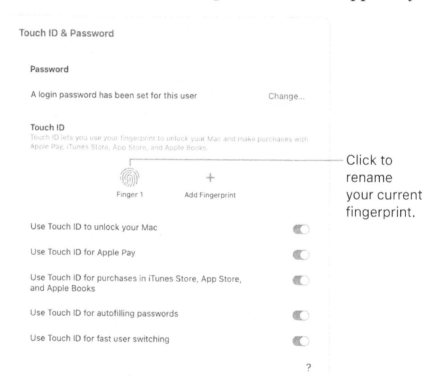

Set up Touch ID

❖ Select Apple menu > Systems Setting, then click the **Touch ID and Password** button on the side bar. (You might have to scroll down.)

❖ Click on the **Add Fingerprint** button, insert your passcode, and then adhere to the directives on your display

The Touch ID sensor can be found at the upper right of the keyboard.

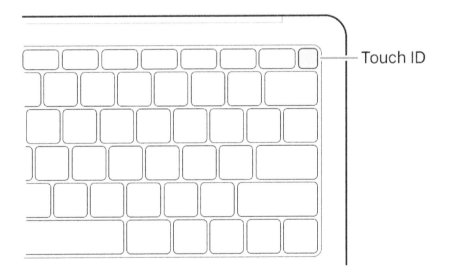

Touch ID

❖ Choose how you want to use Touch ID:
   ➢ Unlock your device
   ➢ Apple Pay
   ➢ Apple Books, iTunes Store, & Apps Store
   ➢ Autofill passwords: You can use Touch ID to automatically insert your username &

passcodes, and automatically insert your credit card info when asked for while making use of Safari & other applications.

➤ Quick user switching: Use the Touch ID feature to switch between user accounts on your device.

Use Touch ID to unlock your Mac

Use Touch ID for Apple Pay

Use Touch ID for purchases in iTunes Store, App Store, and Apple Books

Use Touch ID for autofilling passwords

Use Touch ID for fast user switching

?

Rename or delete fingerprints

❖ Select Apple menu > Systems Setting, then click the **Touch ID and Password** button on the side bar. (You might have to scroll down.)

❖ Carry out any of the below:

➤ Change the name of a fingerprint: Touch the text under the fingerprint, then rename it.

> Erase a fingerprint: Click on one of the fingerprints, type your passcode, click on OK, and then click on the **Delete** button.

Use Touch ID to unlock, sign in, or change users on your Mac

To make use of the Touch ID feature for these functions, you must log in to your MacBook by inserting your passcode.

❖ Unlock your MacBook & other passcode-protected items: After waking your MacBook from sleep or opening password-protected items, simply put your registered finger on the Touch ID sensor when prompted.

❖ Sign in from the sign-in window: Click on your name in the sign-in window, then put your registered finger on the Touch ID sensor.
Only user accounts with passwords can be unlocked with Touch ID. Guest users can't make use of the Touch ID feature.

SIRI

You can use Siri on your device to carry out everyday tasks, such as scheduling meetings, launching applications, or receiving answers to your questions.

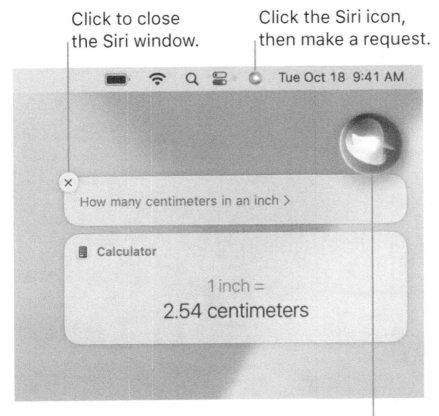

Click to close the Siri window.

Click the Siri icon, then make a request.

Click to make another request.

Activate Siri

❖ Select Apple menu🍎 on your device> Systems Setting, then click on **Siri & Spotlight**🔲 in the side bar. (You might have to scroll down.)

❖ On the right, activate the **Ask Siri** feature if it isn't already enabled, then click on the **Enable** button

Your device has to have internet connection before you can make use of Siri.

❖ When asked if you would like to improve Siri & Dictation, carry out any of the below:

➢ Share Voice Recordings: Click on the **Share Audio Recordings** button to let Apple save Siri & Dictations interactions. Apple can review stored audio samples.

➢ Do not share your voice recordings: Click on the **Not Now** button.

If you later change your mind & would like to share or stop sharing your voice recordings, select Apple menu > Systems Settings, then click on Privacy and Security in the side bar. (You might have to scroll down.) Head over to Analytics and Improvements on the right, then activate or deactivate the Improve Siri and Dictation feature.

❖ Carry out any of the below:

➢ Use the "**Hey Siri**" feature: Activate the **Listen for "Hey Siri"** feature. Then you can say "Hey Siri" to start making use of Siri. If this option is enabled & you activate the "**Allow Siri when locked**" feature, you can make use of Siri when your device is locked or in sleep mode.

➢ Set a keyboard shortcut: Click on the "Keyboard Shortcut" drop-down menu, then select one of the shortcuts to activate Siri or create yours.

❖ Change Siri's voice or language: Click on the Language drop-down menu, then select one of the languages. To listen to a preview, click on the Select button beside Siri Voice, then select the voice you want Siri to use from the available voices

❖ Silent Siri: Click on Siri Response, then disable the **Voice Feedback** feature — Siri responses will be displayed in the Siri window instead of being spoken.

❖ Display what Siri says on your screen: Click on Siri Response, then activate the "**Always show Siri captions**" feature.

❖ Display what you're saying on the screen: Click on Siri Response, then activate the "**Always show speech**" feature.

To get more info about how Apple protects your information & allows you to choose what you share, click on the **Siri Suggestion and Privacy** button, then click on **About Siri and Privacy**.

Tip: To add Siri to the menu bar, select Apple menu > Systems Setting, then click on Controls Centre in the side bar. (You might have to scroll down.) Head over to Menu Bar Only on the right, then select the Show in the Menu Bar option beside Siri.

Summon Siri

Note: Your device has to have internet connection before you can make use of Siri.

❖ To summon Siri, simply carry out any of the below:
   ➢ Click on the Siri button in the menu bar. if it isn't there, you can follow the instructions above to add it to the menu bar.
   ➢ Long-press the Dictation button in the Functions row, or use the keyboard shortcut you created when setting up Siri.
   ➢ Say "Hey Siri"

❖ Request for something—for instance, "What's the weather forecast for today" or "Setup a meeting at 10"

Deactivate Siri

❖ Select Apple menu🍎 on your device> Systems Setting, then click on **Siri & Spotlight** 🔘 in the side bar. (You might have to scroll down.)
❖ On the right, deactivate the **Ask Siri** feature.

Clear Siri & Dictation history

After activating Siri, you can share your Siri & Dictation audio recordings on your device with Apple.

You can erase request history —both transcript & voice recordings—that's less than 6 months old (your device must have an internet connection).

- Select Apple menu on your device> Systems Setting, then click on **Siri & Spotlight** in the side bar. (You might have to scroll down.)
- On the right, click on the **Delete Siri and Dictation History** button
- Click on the **Delete** button

If Siri isn't working as expected

If you have trouble using Siri, try the following suggestions.

- Ensure your MacBook has an Internet connection. Select the Apple menu > Systems Setting, and click Network in the sidebar. (You might have to scroll down.)
- Ensure that you've activated Siri
- Ensure your MacBook microphone isn't obstructed by any object
- If you are making use of an external Mic, check that it is connected to your device, selected in Audio settings and that the input volume is sufficient.

  Select the Apple menu > Systems Setting, click on Sound in the side bar (You might have to scroll down.), click on the **Input** button, and move the "Input Volume" slider.

❖ If you activate the **Listen for Hey Siri** feature, ensure the lid of your MacBook is open before you summon Siri with "Hey Siri".

KEYBOARD SHORTCUTS

One of the most important tools to monitor production in office work is the use of keyboard shortcuts. The right shortcut can turn the keyboard on the typewriter into a command center for your computer.

By clicking on a few combinations, you can often do whatever you normally do with your mouse, trackpad, or other input device, with only your keyboard.

To use the keyboard shortcut, click and hold one or more buttons, and then click the last shortcut key. For instance, to make use of Command-X (cut) hold down the command button, then press the X button, and then release the two buttons. Mac Menus & keyboards often use icons for certain keys, as well as modifiers:

Shift ⇧

Command (Cmd) ⌘

Control (or Ctrl) ^

Options (or Alt) ⌥

Caps Lock ⇪

Fn

Some Apple keyboards have icons and special functions for display brightness ☼, keyboard brightness ☼, Mission Control, and much more.

Learn macOS keyboard shortcuts

You'll find keyboard shortcuts beside menu items in macOS applications.

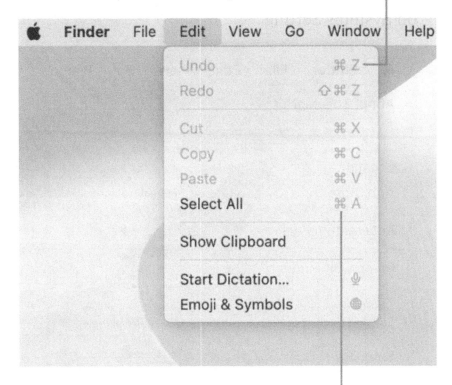

Keyboard shortcuts

Symbols represent
modifier keys.

Personalize keyboard shortcuts

You can change key combinations to personalize
some keyboard shortcuts.

❖ Select Apple menu 🍎 on your device, then click on Systems Setting

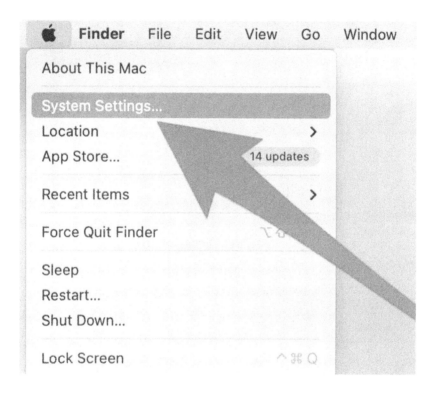

❖ Click on the Keyboard button ⌨ on the side bar, and then click on the **Keyboard Shortcuts** button on the right side of your display.

* Select any of the categories in the list on the left, such as Screenshots or Function Keys.
* Select the check box beside any of the shortcuts you would like to change in the list on the right
* Click the current key combination twice, then enter the new combination.

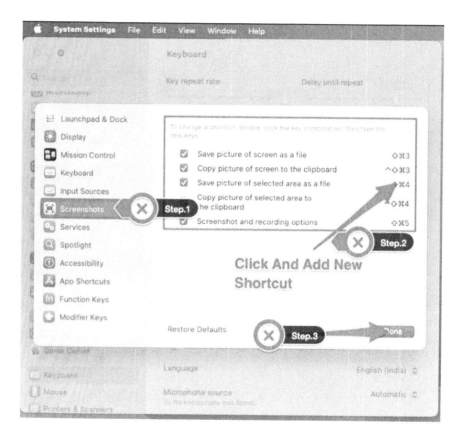

❖ For the new keyboard shortcut to take effect, exit and open the application you are using.

If you assign an existing shortcut to another command or application, your new shortcut would not work. Find the menu command that is making use of it, then reassign the shortcut for that item.

If you want to reset all the shortcuts to their default key combinations, head over to Keyboard Settings, click on the **Keyboard Shortcuts** button, and then click on the **Restore Defaults** button.

Turn off keyboard shortcuts

Sometimes an application's keyboard shortcuts conflict with macOS keyboard shortcuts. If this happens, you can turn off the macOS keyboard shortcut.

❖ Select Apple menu on your device, then click on Systems Setting

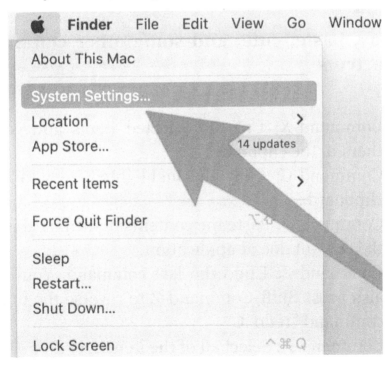

- ❖ Click on the Keyboard button on the side bar, and then click on the **Keyboard Shortcuts** button on the right side of your display.
- ❖ Select any of the categories in the list on the left, such as Screenshots or Function Keys.
- ❖ Deselect the check box beside any of the shortcuts you would like to turn off in the list on the right

Default keyboard shortcuts

Copy, paste, cute, and some other common shortcuts

- ❖ Command-X: Cut the selected items and copy them to the clipboard.
- ❖ Command-C: Copy the highlighted item to the clipboard.
- ❖ Command-V: Paste the contents of the board into the current doc or application.
- ❖ Command-Z: Undo the last command. You can also press Shift-Command-Z to reverse the undo command/ redo it.
- ❖ Command-A: Select all of the items.

- ❖ Command-F: Find something in the doc or open the search window.
- ❖ Command-G: Search again: Look for the next occurrence.
- ❖ Command-H: hide the front application window. Press Option-Command-H to see the front application but hide all the other applications.
- ❖ Command-P: Print the present doc
- ❖ Command-S: Save the current file.
- ❖ Command-T: Opens a new tab.
- ❖ Command-W: Close the window on the front. Press Option-Command-W to close all windows of the application.
- ❖ Option-Command-Esc: force quit an application.
- ❖ Control-Command-F: If it is supported by the application, make use of the application in full screen.
- ❖ Spacebar: Use Quick View to preview selected items.
- ❖ Command-tab: Go to the last used app in all open applications.
- ❖ Shift-Command-5: Take a screenshot or make a screen record. Use Shift-Command-3 or Shift-Command-4 for screenshots.
- ❖ Shift-Command-N: Creates a new folder in Finder.

Documents shortcuts

The format of these shortcuts may vary depending on the application you are making use of.

* Command-I: put the selected text in italics, or undo it.
* Command-K: Adds a web link.
* Command-U: Line or remove selected text, or undo it.
* Command-T: Show or hide the window for fonts.
* Command-D: Select the Desktop folder from the Open dialog box or from the Save dialogue box.
* Shift-Command-Colon (:): Show the window for spelling and grammar.
* Command-Semicolon (;): Find the misspelt words in the doc.
* Fn - Top arrow: to scroll up by a page.
* Fn - Down arrow: scroll down by a page
* Fn - Left Arrow: Home: Slide to the beginning of the doc.
* Fn - Right Arrow: End: Slide to the end of the doc.
* Command - Up arrow: Move the point of insertion to the beginning of the doc.
* Command - Down arrow: Move the point of insertion to the end of the doc.

- Command - Left Arrow: Moves to the point of insertion to the starting of the present line.
- Command - Right Arrow: move the point of insertion to the ending of the present line.
- Options - Left arrow: Move the entry point to the beginning of the previous word.
- Options - Right Arrow: Move the insertion point to the end of the next word.
- Control-A: Slide to the beginning of a line or paragraph.
- Control E: Jump to the end of a paragraph or line.
- Control-F: move by a character forward.
- Control-B: move by a character backwards.
- Shift - Command - Number (-): reduces the size of the selected item.

System and finder shortcut

- Command-D: Duplicate the files you selected.
- Command-E: Remove the selected disk or volume.
- Command-F: Start the search on the spotlight in the Finder window.
- Shift-Command-C: Open the computer window.
- Shift-Command-D: launch the desktop folder.

- ❖ Shift-Command-F: Open the Recents window and show all the files you have recently viewed or modified.
- ❖ Shift-Command-H: Open the Home folder of your current macOS user account.
- ❖ Shift-Command-I: Open iCloud Drive.
- ❖ Shift-Command-K: launch the window of Network.
- ❖ Option-Command-L: launch the download folder.
- ❖ Shift-Command-N: Creates a new folder.
- ❖ Shift-Command-O: Launch the Docs folder.
- ❖ Shift-Command-P: Display or hide the Preview pane of the Finder window.
- ❖ Shift-Command-R: Open the AirDrop window.
- ❖ Shift-Command-T: hide or display the tab bar that is in the finder window.
- ❖ Control-Shift-Command-T: Adds Finder items selected into the dock
- ❖ Shift-Command-U: Open the Utilities folder.
- ❖ Option-command-D: hide or display the dock.
- ❖ Option-command-S: Hide or show the sidebar in the finders window.
- ❖ Command - Slash (/): Hide the status bar or show it in the Finder window.
- ❖ Command-J: Show your view options.

❖ Command-K: Open the Server Connection window.

❖ Command-N: Opens a New Finder window.

❖ Option-Command-N: Create a smart folder.

❖ Command-T: When a single tab in the Finder window opens, it shows or hides the tab bar.

❖ Option-Command-T: Show or hide the toolbar when a single tab opens in the Finder window.

❖ Option-Command-V: Move the clipboard files to the current location from their original location.

❖ Command-Y: Quickly preview selected files using quick look.

❖ Option-Command-Y: Browse the Quick View slideshow for selected files.

❖ Command - Bracket left ([): head over to the previous folder.

❖ Command - Bracket right (]): Go to the next folder.

FACETIME

With FaceTime, you can make voice & video calls from your MacBook to others.

Note: Before you can make use of FaceTime, your device needs to have an internet connection and you have to login to Face-Time with your Apple ID.

Sign in to FaceTime

When you launch the FaceTime application for the first time or after signing out, you will be asked to log in with your Apple ID.

❖ In the Face-Time application, type your Apple ID details in the appropriate fields.
❖ Click on Next to log in

After logging in, you can pick a ringtone, activate features like Live Photo, & configure other settings.

Stop receiving FaceTime calls

If you no longer want to receive FaceTime calls on your Mac, you can log out or turn off FaceTime.

In the Face-Time application, carry out any of the below:

❖ Log out of Face-Time: Select Face-Time, click on Settings in the Menu, click on the **General** button, and then click on Sign Out.

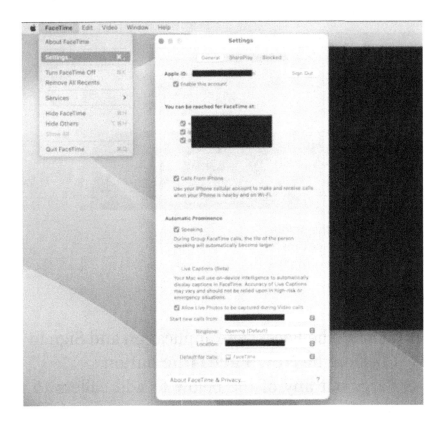

❖ Turn off FaceTime: Select FaceTime, and click on Turn Off FaceTime. Click on Turn On to turn it back on.

Make a FaceTime call on your Mac

Click to hide the call window.

Picture-in-picture window

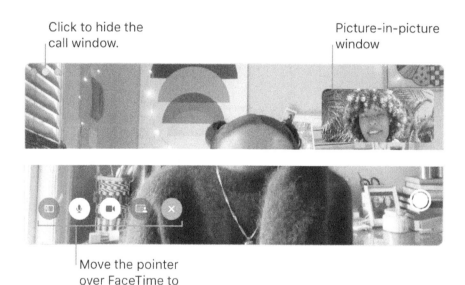

Move the pointer over FaceTime to see call options.

❖ Launch the Face-Time application and Sign in
❖ Click on the **New FaceTime** button
❖ Carry out any of the below to add callers to the New FaceTime window:

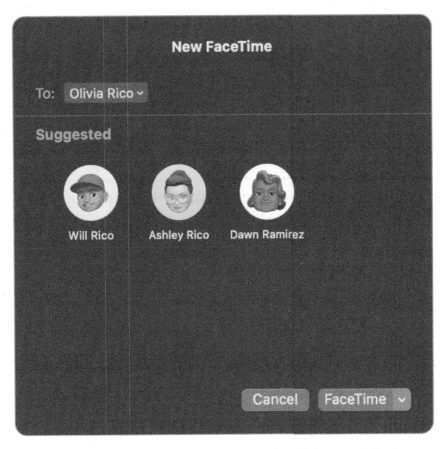

> Type the number or e-mail address of the individual you would like to call. You may need to press Return.
> If you have a card for the individual in the Contacts application, you can type the name of the individual or choose them from the **Suggestions** section.

Note: If someone's name is blue, it means the person has an Apple ID and you can call the person on FaceTime directly—the call will ring on the individual's Apple device. If someone's name is green, you can click "Invite with Messages" to send them a text message with a link. If someone's name is red, it means you can't reach the person with the Messages application.

❖ Click on the **FaceTime** button to begin a Face-Time video call. To start a Face-Time voice call, click on the down arrow ∨ and click on Face-Time Audio.

Make a group Face-Time call

You can have up to thirty-two individuals in a Group Face-Time call.

❖ Launch the Face-Time application and Sign in
❖ Click on the **New FaceTime** button
❖ Carry out any of the below to add callers to the New FaceTime window:
  ➢ Type the number or e-mail address of the individual you would like to call. You may need to press Return.
  ➢ If you have a card for the individual in the Contacts application, you can type the name of

the individual or choose them from the **Suggestions** section.

Note: If someone's name is blue, it means the person has an Apple ID and you can call the person on FaceTime directly—the call will ring on the individual's Apple device. If someone's name is green, you can click "Invite with Messages" to send them a text message with a link. If someone's name is red, it means you can't reach the person with the Messages application.

❖ Repeat the step above till you have listed all participants

❖ Click on the **FaceTime** button to begin a Face-Time video call. To start a Face-Time voice call, click on the down arrow⌄ and click on Face-Time Audio.

Everyone participating in the call will appear in a tile on your display. When somebody starts speaking or you click on a tile, that tile will become more prominent. Scroll down to find a participant you can't see.

To stop the speaker's tile from becoming more prominent during a Group call, Select FaceTime> Settings, click on General, then unselect Speaking in the Automatic Prominence segment.

Add others to a FaceTime call

While on a Face-Time call, you can add more individuals to the call, even if you did not start the call.

❖ While on a call in the FaceTime application

❖ Click on the Sidebar icon ⬚.

❖ Click on the Add icon ⊕, then carry out any of the below:

> Type the number or e-mail address of the individual you would like to call. You may need to press Return.

> If you have a card for the individual in the Contacts application, you can type the name of the individual or choose them from the **Suggestions** section.

Note: If someone's name is blue, it means the person has an Apple ID and you can call the person on FaceTime directly—the call will ring on the individual's Apple device. If someone's name is green, you can click "Invite with Messages" to send them a text message with a link. If someone's name is red, it means you can't reach the person with the Messages application.

❖ Click on the **Add** button

Pause a Face-Time video call

Pause a Face-Time video call to temporarily stop the video stream. If you don't mute the call, both parties will still be able to hear each other. On your MacBook, carry out any of the below:

❖ Pause a video call: Click on the Yellow minimize icon in the upper part of the Face-Time window or switch to another application.
Note: If you are in a group call, the minimize icon will only minimize your screen; it does not pause the FaceTime call.
❖ Click on the Face-Time icon in the Dock to resume a paused video call.

End a call

To end a call in the Face-Time application on your MacBook, carry out any of the below:

❖ End a voice call: Click on the End button.
❖ End a video call: Hover the cursor over the call window, then click on the End Call icon.

After ending a Group call, it will remain active till all participants leave the call. Click on the Join Video icon ⬤ to join it again.

Accept FaceTime calls

❖ Carry out any of the below when a notification pops-up in the upper right corner of your display:
  ➤ Click on the Accept button to accept an incoming call.
  ➤ Accept a video call as a voice call: Click on the down arrow ⌄ beside Accept, then select the **Answer as an Audio** option. The camera turns off automatically when you make a voice call.
  ➤ Accept a call and end the current call: Click on the **End & Accept** button.
  ➤ Accept a voice call & put the current voice call on hold: Click on the **Hold and Accept** button. When the new call ends, the waiting call resumes.
  ➤ Join a Face-Time group call: Click on the **Join** button, then click on the Join Video icon ⬤ in the Face-Time window.

Reject a Face-Time call

Send a text message or create a reminder.

Carry out any of the below when a notification pops-up in the upper right corner of your display:

❖ Click on the Decline button to reject an incoming call.
The caller will see that you are unavailable for a call.
❖ Decline a call & send a message via iMessage: Click on the down arrow ⌄ beside Decline, then select the Reply with Message option, type the message, and then click on the **Send** button.
❖ Decline a call and set a reminder to call later: Click on the down arrow ⌄ beside Decline, then select when you would like to receive the reminder. You'll get a notification when it's time - click to see the reminder, then click on the link in the reminder to start the FaceTime call.

Return recent or missed calls from Face-Time

You can find all the calls you have received or made on the left side of the Face-Time window (unless you've cleared your call history).

List of recent calls

❖ In the Face-Time application, hover the cursor over the call window, and then click on the Voice Call button 📞 or the Video Call button 📹 next to a call

Return a call in another way

Carry out any of the below on your MacBook:

❖ Return a missed call from the Notifications Centre: Click on the time & date in the menu bar at the upper part of your display to view notifications, and then click on a call in the missed calls list.
❖ Return a call from the dock: Ctrl-click on the Face-Time icon, then click on one of the calls under Recent Calls.

Create & share a Face-Time link

You can create a FaceTime call link and share it with others whether they are using an Apple device or not. As the originator of the link, you have to start the call and allow others to join.

- ❖ Enter the Face-Time application and sign in(if you haven't).
- ❖ Click on the **Create Link** button
- ❖ Choose one of the sharing options. For instance, select Messages to send a text message to the person that includes the Face-Time call link.

Start a FaceTime call from the link

If you've created a Face-Time call link, you can start the call from an application (for instance, click on **Join** in a Message conversation) or from Face-Time. If the link was created a few days ago, you'll see the link in the recent calls list in the Upcoming segment; otherwise, you can find it in the date-based segment- for instance, under Last Week.

- ❖ In the Face-Time application, hover the cursor over the call window and look for the call made with a Face-Time link, then click on the Video icon .
- ❖ Click on the **Join** button

Allow callers to join Face-Time calls

The Face-Time link originator can allow others to join the call. Other callers (those that are making use of Apple devices, who have been authenticated and joined the Face-Time call for about thirty seconds) can also accept (or decline) the request to join the call.

You know a new caller is waiting when a badge pops-up on the side bar icon .

❖ When making a call in the Face-Time application on your MacBook, click on the Sidebar icon when the badge pops up.
❖ Carry out any of the below:
  ➢ Allow the individual to join the call: Click on Approve Join Request .
  ➢ Do not let the individual join the call: Click on Decline Join Request .

To disable the sound alert when someone tries to join the call, click on the sidebar icon , and then select **Silence Join Request**.

Delete a Face-Time link

If you don't need a Face-Time link you created anymore, you can delete it.

❖ In the Face-Time application, view the list of callers for the call made through a Face-Time link.

❖ Click on the Details icon ⓘ and then click on the **Delete Link** button.

Join a call on your MacBook from a Face-Time link

After receiving a FaceTime call link, you can join the call using your MacBook.

❖ Click on the Face-Time call link, then click on the **Join** button in the Face-Time application.
If you are the Face-Time link originator, the call will begin. The Face-Time link originator can allow you to join the call; the connection creator may allow you to join the call immediately; other callers (those that are making use of Apple devices, who have been authenticated and joined the Face-Time call for about thirty seconds) can also accept (or decline) requests to join the call.

Join a call on a Windows or Android device from a Face-Time link

❖ Touch or click on the Face-Time call link.
❖ Type your name to join the Face-Time call, then touch or click on the **Continue** button.
   When you first join a Face-Time call on your device, you may need to let Face-Time gain access to your camera & Mic.
❖ Touch or click on the **Join** button.

   The Face-Time link originator can allow you to join the call; the connection creator may allow you to join the call immediately; other callers (those that are making use of Apple devices, who have been authenticated and joined the Face-Time call for about thirty seconds) can also accept (or decline) requests to join the call.

To end the call, touch or click on the **Leave** button in the lower left corner of your display.

Manage FaceTime calls on the web

After joining a Face-Time call from a link, you can share the link with other people; change your view, etc.

When making a Face-Time call over the Internet, carry out any of the below:

❖ Make a video call in full screen: Touch or click on the Toggle Full-Screen icon .

❖ Go back to normal window size: Touch or click on the Toggle Full-Screen icon or press the Esc button.

❖ Switch to a voice call: Touch or click on the Mute Video icon . Touch or click the icon once more to turn on the camera.

❖ Mute a call: Touch or click on the Mute icon . You'll still be able to hear what the other person is saying but they would be unable to hear you.
Touch or click on the Mute icon once more to unmute yourself.

❖ Arrange participants in a grid: Touch or click on the **Grid** button at the upper part of the window.

❖ Share the FaceTime link with others: Touch or click on the More Options icon , select Share Link or Copy Link, and then select how you want the link to be shared.

❖ Change your MIC or camera: Touch or click on the More Options icon , then select the Microphone or Camera you would like to use.

Use SharePlay to share your screen on FaceTime

The SharePlay feature allows MacBook users to share their display to show applications, web pages, and more while on a Face-Time video call. You can look through photo albums together, or receive feedbacks on what you are working on while seeing & hearing each other's reactions.

❖ When making a Face-Time call on your MacBook, open an application you would like to share in the call.

❖ Click on the Face-Time button in the menu bar.

❖ Click on the Share Display icon , then carry out any of the below:

  ➢ Share application window: Select Window, hover the cursor over the application you would like to share, and then click on Share This Window.

  ➢ Share the entire screen: Select Screen, hover the cursor to anywhere on your display, then click on Share This Screen.

To stop sharing your display, click on the FaceTime icon in the menu bar and click on **Stop Sharing**.

Take Live Photos on FaceTime

While on a Face-Time video call, you can capture a live photo with a participant in the call. The two of you'll receive an alert that the picture was taken, and the Live Picture will be added to the Photo library.

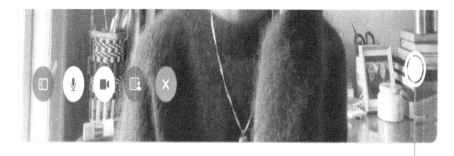

Live Photo button

Setup FaceTime for Live Pictures

❖ In the Face-Time application, select FaceTime Settings and then click on the **General** button

❖ Select the "Allow Live Photo to be captured during video call" check box.

When you tick the checkbox, you are also permitting other people to take Live Photos of you.

Setup Photos For Live Photos

❖ Launch the Photos application if you have not opened the application before.

Capture a Live Photo

❖ During a video call in the FaceTime application, carry out any of the below:
  ➢ On a single call: Select the Face-Time window.
  ➢ On a group call: Double-click the person's tile
❖ Click on the Capture icon ○.
  An alert will tell you that you've taken a Live Photo.
❖ In the Photos application ◉ , browse & checkout pictures to see the Live Photo.

Mute or change FaceTime call volume

During a FaceTime call, carry out any of the below:

❖ Mute yourself: In the Face-Time application, hover the cursor over the call window, then click on the Mute icon 🎤 . You'll still be able to hear what the other person is saying but they would be unable to hear you.
Click on the Mute icon once more to unmute yourself.

❖ Change your microphone volume: Select Apple menu > Systems Setting, click on the Sound 🔊 button in the sidebar, head over to Output & Input on the right side of the window, click on the **Input** button, and then drag the "Input Volume" slider.

Filter out background sounds

If you want others in the FaceTime call to hear your voice clearly and background sounds filtered out, you can activate the Voice Isolation feature. This feature makes your voice the priority on a call & filters out background noise.

ears when you're
FaceTime call.

Depending on your Mac,
you can change the
video or audio effects.

* While on a call in the FaceTime application, click on Controls Centre ⌥ in the menu bar, and then click Mic Mode.
* Click on Voice Isolation

If you want those on the call to hear your voice & the background sound, you can simply select Wide Spectrum.

Enable or disable Portrait mode

Portrait mode blurs the background & places the visual focus on you.

During a FaceTime video call, carry out any of the below:

❖ Click on Controls Centre in the menu bar, click on Video Effects, and then click on Portrait.

ears when you're
FaceTime call.

Depending on your Mac,
you can change the
video or audio effects.

❖ Click on your tile, and then click on the Video Effect icon 👤 .
Touch the icon once more to deactivate Portrait mode.

Activate Live Captions in FaceTime

During a video call, you can activate Live Captions (Beta version) to see the discussion transcribed on your display. If you have trouble hearing the conversation, the Live Captions feature can make it very easy to follow along.

❖ While on a video call in the Face-Time application, select Live Captions in the side bar.
If you can't find the side bar, click on the sidebar icon 🗔 at the lower part of the window.
❖ If prompted, click on the **Download** button.

To deactivate the Live Captions feature, simply unselect Live Captions in the side bar.

Change or turn off all notifications from Face-Time

You can control what kind of notifications you get for Face-Time calls, or you can turn off notifications entirely.

❖ Select Apple menu💥 > Systems Settings, then click on the Notification 🔲 button in the side bar
❖ Click on FaceTime on the right side of the window, then carry out any of the below:
  ➢ Change notifications: Set options like how notifications are displayed or where to display the notifications. Click on the Help icon ? at the lower part of the window to get more information about the options.
  ➢ Disable "Allow notifications" to turn off all notifications from Face-Time.

Change FaceTime ringtones

❖ In the FaceTime application, select FaceTime> Settings and then click on the **General** button
❖ Click on Ringtone drop-down menu, then select a ringtone.

Block FaceTime callers

If you do not want to receive Face-Time calls from certain individuals on your MacBook, you can block them.

❖ In the FaceTime application, select FaceTime> Settings and then click on the **Blocked** button
❖ Click on the Add icon ┼, then select one of the names from the contacts list.

To unblock someone, select the person's name, and then click on the Remove icon ─.

Delete your FaceTime call history

Carry out any of the below in the FaceTime application:

❖ Delete a specific call: Ctrl-click on the call, then select Remove from Recent.
❖ Remove all recent calls: Select FaceTime> Remove All Recent.

Keyboard shortcuts in FaceTime

In the Face-Time application on your MacBook, you can do many things quickly using keyboard shortcuts.

Note: Cmd stands for command

- ❖ Cmd-Comma(,): Open Face-Time settings
- ❖ Option-Command-H: Hide everything except for Face-Time
- ❖ Cmd-H: Hide FaceTime
- ❖ Cmd-Q: Quit FaceTime
- ❖ Cmd-K: Turn off Facetime
- ❖ Cmd-R: Use portrait or landscape while on a video call
- ❖ Ctrl- Cmd-F: Enter or leave full-screen while on a video call
- ❖ Cmd-M: Minimize windows
- ❖ Cmd-W: Close the window

MAIL

Mail allows you to manage all your e-mail accounts in one application.

Add an email account in Mail

❖ When you launch the Mail application for the first time, you may be told to add an account. Choose one of the account types (like, iCloud) or the **Other Mail Account** option, and then fill in your account details.

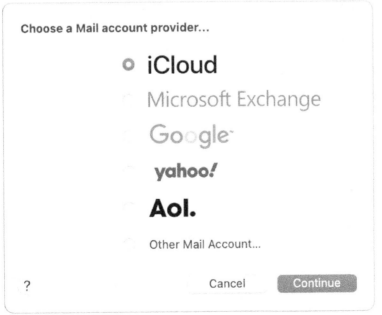

❖ If you've already added an e-mail account, you can add more. In the Mail application, select Mail> Add Account, choose one of the account types, and then fill in your account details.

Sign out of or temporarily disable an e-mail account

You can temporarily stop making use of an e-mail account in the Mail application, and then activate it again when you are ready. If you disable an account, its messages will not appear in the Mail application.

❖ In the Mail application, select Mail > Account.
❖ Select the account you plan to disable and then unselect the Mail checkbox.

When you are ready to use the account again, simply select the account's mail check box.

Sign out or remove an email account

When you remove an e-mail account, the account's e-mail messages will be removed from your device.

❖ In the Mail application, select Mail> Settings and then click on the **Accounts** button.

❖ Select one of the accounts, then click on the Remove icon —

Write & send an email

Add text, photos, and files, or mark up attachments.

Click to send email later.

Add address fields like Cc or Bcc.

Add people from Contacts.

To: Antonio Manriquez ˅

Cc:

Subject: Remember this?

Message Size: 1.9 MB   Image Size: Actual Size

Hi Antonio — Thought you'd enjoy this memory from our afternoon in Golden Gate Park. The flowers were gorgeous!

Danny

- ❖ In the Mail application, click on the Compose icon 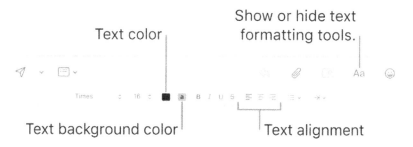 in the Mail tool bar.
- ❖ In your message, type the name(s) or e-mail address in one of the address fields (like To or Cc).

  While typing, the Mail application will display addresses you've used in the past or that it finds in the Contacts application.

  Or, click on an address field, and then click on the Add icon ⊕ that pops-up. Click on one of the contacts in the list, then click on the e-mail address.
- ❖ To use other fields, like Priority or Bcc, click on the Header icon ⊡∨, then click on the field.
- ❖ Type the subject of the e-mail, and then write what you have in mind.

  You can carry out any of the below:

Show or hide text formatting tools.

Text color

Times   16   ▣ a   B I U S ≡ ≡ ≡ ≡ ∨ →∨   Aa ☺

Text background color

Text alignment

  - ➤ Click on the Formatting icon Aa to change styles & fonts.

> Click on the Emoji icon 😄 to add a symbol or emoji
> Translate Text: Highlight the text, Ctrl-click the selected text, and then select Translate. From the drop-down menu select the languages you want to translate from & to.

❖ Click on the Send icon 🛪 to send the email

Schedule an email with the Send Later feature

In Mail, click on the drop-down menu beside the Send icon 🛪 , then select one of the options.

E-mails you decided to send later will appear in the Send Later mail box in the side bar.

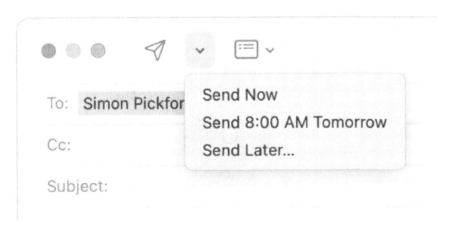

Unsend e-mails with Undo Send

If you made a mistake in your email or sent the wrong email, you can recall the e-mail with the Undo Send feature. You can also increase the delay time for e-mails to give yourself more time to unsend e-mails.

❖ In the Mail application, click on the **Undo Send** button at the lower part of the side bar within ten seconds of sending an e-mail (or select Edit, then click on Undo).

Click to search for an item in Mail.

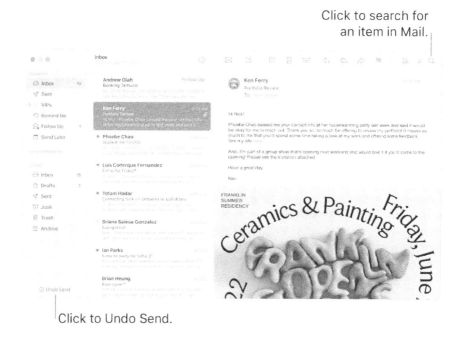

Click to Undo Send.

Note: To increase or reduce the time you have to unsend an email or to disable the Undo Send feature, select Mail> Settings, click on Composing, click on the **Undo send delay** drop-down menu, and then select one of the options.

Add pictures & other files in e-mails

When writing a message in the Mail application on your MacBook, carry out any of the below:

❖ Click on the Attachment icon in the tool bar, look for the file, select it, and then click on **Choose File**.

❖ For pictures, click on the Photos icon in the tool bar, then drag one of the pictures into your e-mail.

Reply or forward e-mails

❖ Select one of the messages from the message list by moving the cursor over it and then clicking the message.

To add only a part of the original message in the reply, select the text you would like to add.

❖ Hover the cursor over the message header, then click on any of the icons below:

➤ The Reply icon to reply only to the sender.

➤ The Reply All icon to reply to the sender & other people

➤ The Forward icon to select new recipients

❖ Type your reply

❖ If the original message has an attachment, you can choose to add it or not:

➤ Add attachments: Click on the Insert Attachment icon in the message window toolbar, or select Edit > Attachment > Add Original Attachment to Reply.

➤ Remove attachments: Click on the Remove Attachment icon in the message window toolbar, or select Messages> Remove Attachment.

❖ Click on the Send icon when you are done.

Use Remind Me to come back to e-mails later

If you're too busy at the moment & can't respond to an e-mail, you can set a time you will like to receive a reminder and push the e-mail back to the top of your inbox.

❖ Select the message by moving the cursor over it and then clicking the message, after that use two of your fingers to swipe right on the trackpad, and then click on the **Remind Me** button. Or, Ctrl-click on the message.
❖ Select when you will like to receive a reminder from the menu that appears.

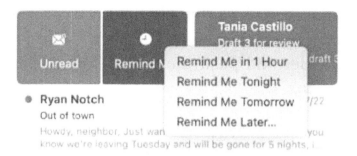

You'll receive a notification for the email, and it will move to the top of your inbox. You can also find the email in the Remind Me mailbox in the side bar.

View e-mail attachments

❖ Select any of the messages that have attachments.
   In the message list, look for the Attachment button under the date you received the message.
❖ Carry out any of the below in the message:
   ➢ Double-click an attachment to open it.
   ➢ Preview the attachment without having to open it: Force-click the attachment (To force-click means to press firmly on your MacBook trackpad till you feel a deep click).

Some attachments—for example, pictures or single-page PDF docs—are shown directly in the email. If you would prefer to view the attachment as an icon, simply Ctrl-click on it, then select the **View as Icon** option from the menu.

Save e-mail attachments

❖ Hover your cursor over a message header
❖ Click on the Attachment icon✎ that appears, click on the attachment's name or select Save All, and then select one of the locations.
❖ Click on the Save button.

Delete attachments

❖ Select one of the messages that have attachments in them by moving the cursor over it and then clicking the message.
❖ Choose Messages, then click on Remove Attachment.

Delete an e-mail

❖ In the Mail application, select the message by moving the cursor over it and then clicking the message.

❖ Click on the Trash icon 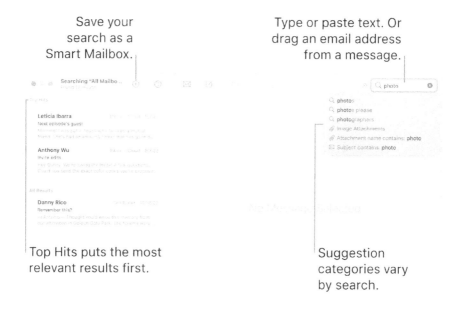 in the tool bar or hover the cursor over the header of the message, then click on Delete when it appears.

Search for emails

After clicking on a search box, smart search suggestions will provide suggested searches and display related content.

Save your search as a Smart Mailbox.

Type or paste text. Or drag an email address from a message.

Top Hits puts the most relevant results first.

Suggestion categories vary by search.

❖ In the Mail application, type a word or phrase in the search box in the toolbar (if it doesn't appear, click on the Search icon $\mathbb{Q}$ in the tool bar).
❖ Press Return
❖ When you are done, click on the Clear icon⊗ in the search box.

Use Mail Privacy Protection

You can activate Mail Privacy Protection to make it difficult for senders to get info about your email activities. To protect e-mail privacy, it hides your IP address from the sender, so that they cannot link it to your other online activities or pinpoint your location. It also stops e-mail senders from knowing if you have opened the e-mail they sent to you.

If you did not activate the Protect Mail Activity feature the first time you launched the Mail application, you can activate it in Mail settings.

❖ In the Mail application, Select Mail> Settings and then click on the **Privacy** button.
❖ Select Protect Mails activity.

SAFARI

The Safari browser is loved for its performance, privacy protections, & power efficiency.

Visit a site using Safari

With the Safari application, it is easy to access the websites you love.

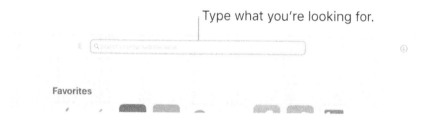

Type what you're looking for.

Favorites

* ❖ In the Safari application, type the name of the website or URL in the Search box.
  Safari suggestions will appear as you type.
* ❖ Select one of the suggestions or press the **Return** button to go to the address you entered.

Personalize your start page. The Start page can display your Favourites, privacy reports, Reading

List items, etc. You can use one of your personal pictures as the background image or use any of the backgrounds provided. To customize your start page, click on the Customize Safari icon at the lower right part of the start page, and select any of the options in the menu.

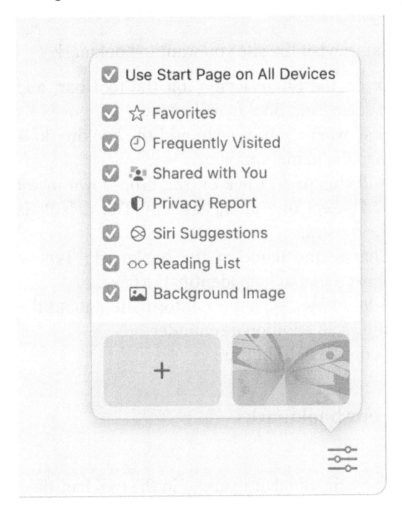

Bookmark sites you would like to revisit

Bookmarks are links to websites that you save so you can quickly revisit the sites later.

Add a bookmark

❖ In Safari, visit the site you want to bookmark.
❖ Click on the Share icon on the tool bar, and then select Add Bookmark.
❖ Choose where you want to add the bookmark, & change the name(optional).
  ➤ Add this page: Click on the drop-down menu and select one of the folders. The default is Favourites.
  ➤ Change the name of the bookmark: Type a short name to help identify the page.
  ➤ Add a note: Type more information about the site as an additional reminder.
❖ Click on the **Add** button.

Find your bookmarks

❖ Click on the Sidebar icon in the tool bar, then click on Bookmarks.

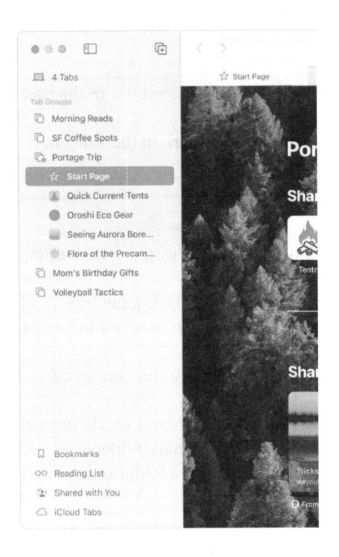

❖ Type the name of the bookmark in the search box at the upper part of the side bar.

You may need to scroll to bring out the search box.

Use a bookmark

❖ Click on the Sidebar icon ⬚ in the tool bar, then click on Bookmarks.
❖ Click on the bookmark in the side bar

Manage bookmarks

❖ Click on the Sidebar icon ⬚ in the tool bar, then click on Bookmarks.
❖ Ctrl-click on one of the bookmarks or folders.
❖ Select from the shortcut menu to carry out any of the below:
  ➢ Edit or change the name of a folder or bookmark
  ➢ Edit the site address of a bookmark.
  ➢ Create a bookmark folder
  ➢ Delete or copy a folder or bookmark
  ➢ And more

To change the description of a bookmark, double-click one of the folders on the sidebar, then Ctrl-click the item and select Edit Description.

Use tabs

Avoid cluttering your desktop with multiple windows when you are browsing or researching a topic. Instead, you can browse multiple web pages in one Safari window using tabs.

Open a new tab

❖ In Safari, click on the New Tab icon ╈ on the tool bar.

Preview a tab

❖ In Safari, simply move the cursor over a tab to preview it.

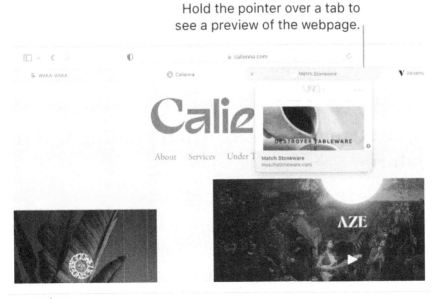

Hold the pointer over a tab to see a preview of the webpage.

Open a web page in a new tab

Carry out any of the below in the Safari application:

❖ Cmd-click on a link on the website.

❖ Cmd-click the Forward icon ⟩ or the Back icon ⟨ to open the next or previous page in another tab.

Open a tab in another window

❖ In Safari, select Window> Move Tab to a New Window.

Reopen a recently closed tab

In Safari, select History > Recently Closed, and then select the website you would like to reopen.

Hide advertisements when reading text in Safari

The **Safari Reader** feature allows you to see a website article on a single-page without advertisements, navigation, or other distractions.

You can change the style & size of the font, & the background colour.

View articles using Reader

❖ In Safari, click on the Reader icon ⬚ in the Search field.

The icon will only appear if the page has an article that supports the Reader feature.
❖ Click on the Reader icon once more or Press Esc to leave Reader mode.

Change how webpages look in Reader

❖ While going through an article in Readers view, click on the Format icon AA in the right end of the Search bar.
❖ Carry out any of the below to change the settings:
  ➢ Select one of the font sizes
  ➢ Select a background colour
  ➢ Select one of the fonts.

Translate a webpage

When you come across a webpage that is in another language, you can use Safari to translate it to the language you understand.

❖ Click on the Translate icon on the webpage, and then select a language.

Check the items you've downloaded

❖ In Safari, click on the Downloads icon close to the upper right edge of the Safari window.
You won't see the icon if the downloads list is empty.
❖ Carry out any of the below:
  ➢ Pause what you're downloading: Click on the Stop icon in the filename. Click the Continue icon to resume the download.
  ➢ Clear the download list: Click on the **Clear** button in the download list. To remove an item, Ctrl-click the item, then click on Remove From the List.

Save a picture from a website

- Ctrl-click a picture in the Safari application.
- Select the Add Image to Photo, Save Images As, or Save Image to Downloads options.

Interact with the text in an image

The Live Text feature allows you to interact with the text in an image, for instance, you can get a map of an address found in a picture or send an e-mail to an e-mail address you found on a picture online.

- ❖ In Safari, navigate to a picture that contains text. The text could be an e-mail address, a site address, a phone number, an address to a location (like a street address), or words.
- ❖ Hover the cursor over the text, then drag to highlight the text.
- ❖ Ctrl-click on the text you've selected, then select any of the options from the menu that appears.

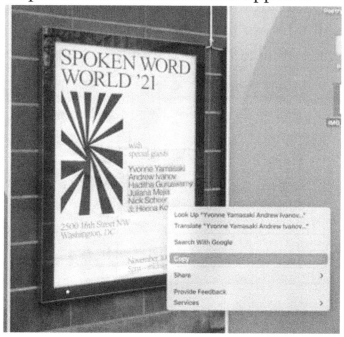

Allow or block pop-ups in Safari

Pop-ups can be useful or annoying. Some sites require you to allow pop-ups. For instance, a bank's site may display your monthly statement in a pop-up. Other sites may fill your display with pop-up advertisements.

You can choose to block or allow popups on individual sites or all sites.

Block or allow pop-ups on a site

❖ In the Safari application, visit the site.
❖ Select Safari> Settings, then click on the **Websites** button.

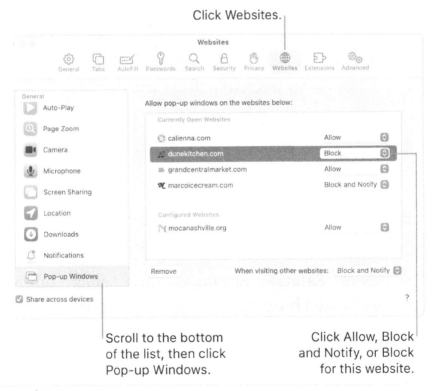

Click Websites.

Scroll to the bottom of the list, then click Pop-up Windows.

Click Allow, Block and Notify, or Block for this website.

- ❖ Click on Pop-ups Windows on the left side of your display. (You may have to scroll down)
- ❖ In the drop-down menu for the site, select any of the below:
  - ➢ Allow.
  - ➢ Block & Notify: Pop-ups for the site will not appear, but when enter a site with blocked pop-ups, you can show the pop-ups by clicking the Display Pop-ups icon 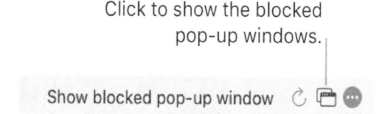 in the Search box.

Click to show the blocked
pop-up windows.

Show blocked pop-up window ↻ 🗗 ⬤

  - ➢ Block.

Block or allow pop-ups on all sites

- ❖ Select Safari> Settings, then click on the **Websites** button.

Click Remove to clear selections
from Configured Websites and
choose another setting.

Click Websites.

Scroll to the bottom
of the list, then click
Pop-up Windows.

Choose the default
setting for all websites
that aren't listed below
Configured Websites.

❖ Click on Pop-ups Windows on the left side of
your display. (You may have to scroll down)

❖ If there are sites listed under Configured Sites,
and you want to make changes to the settings for
these websites (for instance, they are set to
Allow, but you want them to Block pop-ups),
select each site and then click on the **Remove**
button.

❖ Click on the "When visiting other websites" drop-down menu, then select any of the below:
  ➢ Allow.
  ➢ Block & Notify: Pop-ups for the site will not appear, but when you enter a site with blocked pop-ups, you can show the pop-ups by clicking the Display Pop-ups icon in the Search box.
  ➢ Block.

Clear your browsing history

You can delete all logs that Safari keeps of your browsing history

❖ In Safari, select History> Clear History, and then click on the drop-down menu.
❖ Select how much browsing history you want to delete.

Private browsing

When you use private browsing, your browsing data is not saved and the sites you enter are not shared with other Apple devices.

Private window | Normal window

- ❖ In Safari, select File> New Private Window or switch to an already open private window.
  The window will have a dark search box with white text.

Private window

- ❖ Browse as usual.
- ❖ When you are done, close the window, switch to a non-private window, or select File> New Window to open a non-private window.
- ❖ To further improve your privacy, carry out any of the below:
  - ➢ Delete the files you downloaded when making use of private browsing
  - ➢ Close other private windows that are still open to prevent others from gaining access to them.

APPLE PAY

Shop online easily, securely and privately with Apple Pay on your MacBook Air. When shopping online in the Safari application, look for the Apple Pay payment option, click on it, and then confirm your payment with Touch ID.

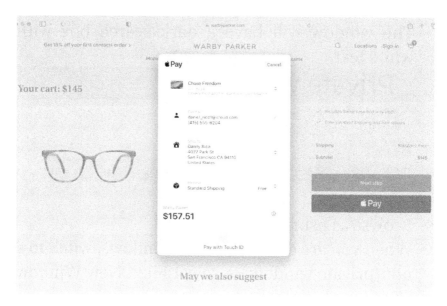

Add a credit or debit card for Apple Pay

❖ Select Apple menu ⬤ > Systems Setting, then click on the **Wallet and Apple Pay** button.

❖ Click on the **Add Card** button on the right
❖ Adhere to the directives on your display to add a card
❖ Verify your info with your card issuer or bank. They may ask for more info.

Use Apple Pay to pay for items online or in applications

❖ When you see Apple Pay as a payment option, click on the Apple Pay button or select Apple Pay as a means of payment.

❖ If you want to pay with another card, simply click on the Next icon ⟩ or the pop-up menu ⌄ beside the default card.

❖ If needed, insert your contact, shipping, & billing details. Apple Pay saves this info, so you don't have to enter it again.

❖ Confirm payment: Adhere to the directives on the display & authenticate with Touch ID

❖ When the payment is complete, you will see Done & a checkmark on your display.

Change your default card

The 1st card you add to Apple Wallet on your MacBook will automatically become your default card. You can change your default card after adding more cards.

❖ Select Apple menu > Systems Setting, then click on the **Wallet and Apple Pay** button.
❖ Select one of the cards from the menu

Remove a card

❖ Select Apple menu > Systems Setting, then click on the **Wallet and Apple Pay** button.
❖ Click on the card you plan on removing.
❖ Click on the Remove icon ⎯ .

Update your Apple Pay billing info

Select Apple menu , click on Systems Setting, click on the **Wallet and Apple Pay** button, and click on one of the cards> Billing Address menu.

Update your Apple Pay contact info

Select Apple menu, click on Systems Setting, click on the **Wallet and Apple Pay** button> click on Contacts & Shipping, and change your e-mail, number, & your shipping address.

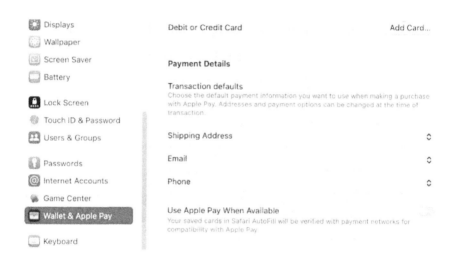

VOICE MEMOS

With Voice memos, you can record song ideas, interviews, class lectures, and more.

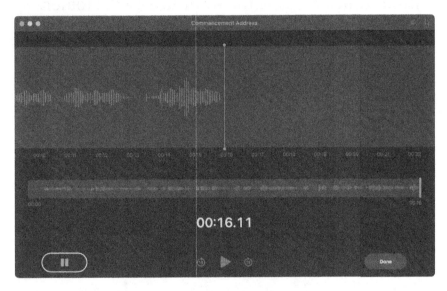

Record from your device: Click on the Record icon to record, then click on **Done** to stop recording. You can change the name of a recording so that you can easily identify it. Click on the name, then type another name. Click on the Play icon to play what you've recorded.

Organize with folders: Create folders to keep your voice memos well arranged. To create a folder, click on the Side bar icon 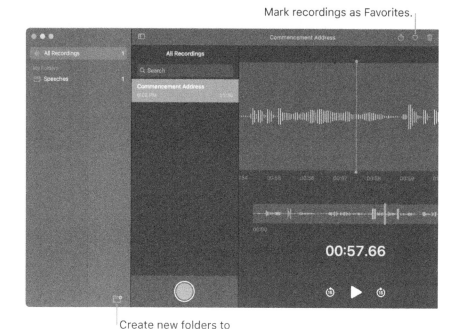 and then click on the **New Folder** icon at the lower part of the side bar. Type a name, then click on the **Save** button. To add a recording to the folder, hold down the Option button while dragging the recording to the folder.

Mark recordings as Favorites.

Create new folders to organize your recordings.

Make a recording as a favourite: Select one of the recordings, then click on the Favourite icon ♡ in the tool bar so that you can find the recording with ease when you need it. Click on the Side Bar icon ⬚ to view all your favourites.

Change the tempo of the song: Increase or decrease the audio speed. Click on the Playback Settings button at the upper part of the Voice Memo window and move the slider.

Improve a recording: Improve the quality of Voice Memos by decreasing background sound & room noise. Click on the Playback Settings button at the upper part of the Voice Memo window and activate Enhance Recordings.

USE YOUR MACBOOK WITH OTHER APPLE DEVICES

Handoff

The Hand-off feature allows you to start something on one of your Apple devices (MacBook, Apple watch, iPad, or iPhone) and pick it up on another Apple device seamlessly. For instance, you can start replying to an e-mail on your iPad, and complete it in the Mail application on your MacBook Air. You can use Hand-off in a lot of Apple applications, such as Safari, Mail, Contacts, & Calendar and some 3rd party applications.

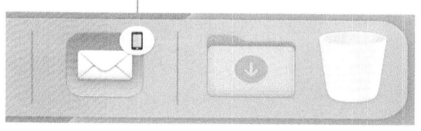

Click to continue what you were doing on your iPhone.

To use the Handoff feature, you have to activate Handoff, Bluetooth, & Wifi on your MacOS, iPadOS, & iOS devices. You must also ensure that both devices are using the same Apple ID.

Enable or disable Handoff

❖ On your MacBook Air: Select Apple menu > Systems Setting, click on the **General** button in the side bar, click on AirDrop and Handoff on the right side of the window, then enable or disable **Allow Hand-off between Mac & your iCloud devices**.

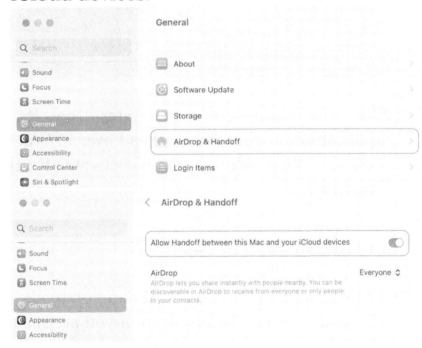

❖ On your iPhone or iPad: Enter the Settings application, touch General> AirPlay and Handoff, and then activate or deactivate the Handoff feature.

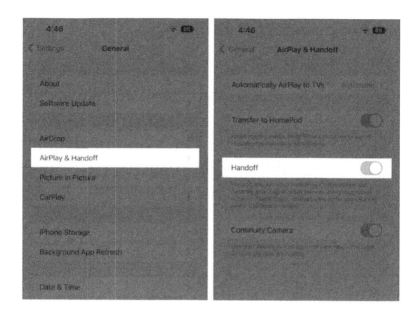

❖ On your Apple Watch: Enter the Watch application on your phone, head over to Watch> General, then activate or deactivate **Enable Handoff**.

Hand off between devices

❖ From your MacBook to an iPhone or iPad: The Handoff icon for the application you are making use of on your MacBook will appear on your iPhone at the lower part of the application switcher or your iPad at the end of the Dock. Touch the Handoff button to continue using the application.

❖ From an iPad, Apple Watch, or iPhone to your MacBook Air: You will find the Handoff icon of the application you are using on your Apple

Watch, iPad, or iPhone close to the right end of the Dock. Click on the icon to continue using the application.

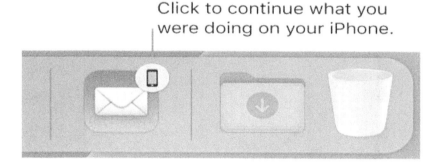

Or, press Cmd-Tab to quickly enter the application that has the Hand-off icon.

Universal Clipboard

Universal Clipboard allows you to Copy the content (videos, text, & pictures) from one of your Apple devices & paste it in another Apple device. For instance, you can copy an article from your MacBook Air & paste it into a note on your iPad. Or copy files from your MacBook Air & paste them into a folder on an iMac.

To use the Universal Clipboard feature, you have to activate Handoff, Bluetooth, & Wifi on your MacOS, iPadOS, & iOS devices. You must also ensure that both devices are using the same Apple ID. Both devices have to be close to each other.

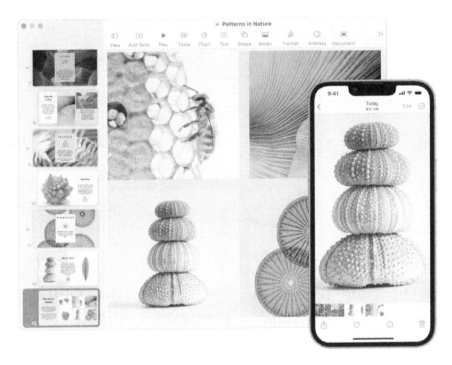

Enable or disable Handoff

❖ On your MacBook Air: Select Apple menu > Systems Setting, click on the **General** button in the side bar, click on AirDrop and Handoff on the right side of the window, then enable or disable

"Allow Hand-off between Mac & your iCloud devices".

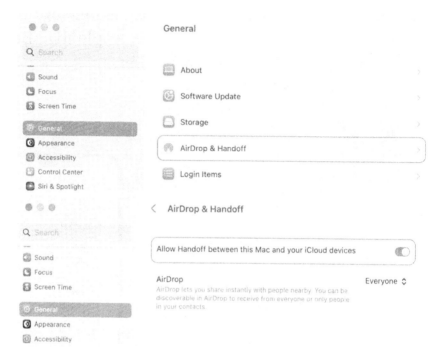

❖ On your iPhone or iPad: Enter the Settings application, touch General> AirPlay and Handoff, and then activate or deactivate the Handoff feature.

Use Universal Clipboard

❖ Copy: Select what you want to copy, and then copy it. For instance, on your MacBook, press Cmd-C or select Edit, then click on Copy.

You have a short time to paste the item you copied

❖ Paste: Hover the cursor to where you want to paste what you've copied, then paste it. For instance, on your iPhone or iPad, double–tap where you want to paste the content on your screen, then touch paste. Or on your MacBook, press Cmd-V to paste what you've copied.

Sidecar

The Sidecar feature allows you to use your iPad as your MacBook's second screen. Like any secondary screen, you can expand your desktop by displaying different windows or applications on your iPad, or mirror what is displayed on your MacBook Air.

To use the Sidecar feature, you have to activate Bluetooth, & Wifi on your devices. You must also ensure that both devices are using the same Apple ID.

Setup Sidecar

❖ Select Apple menu🍎> Systems Setting, then click on the Display⚙ button on the side bar. (You might have to scroll down.)

❖ Click on the Add icon⁺ drop-down menu on the right side of the window, and select your iPad.

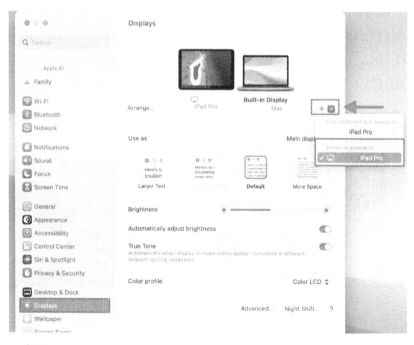

You can also setup Sidecar from the Controls Centre. Click on the Controls Centre icon ⬚ in the menu bar, click on Screen Mirroring, and then select the iPad.

After setting up Sidecar, you will see the Screen Mirroring menu ⬚ in the menu bar. You can change the way you work with your iPad at any time from the Screen Mirroring menu. For instance, you can switch between using your tablet as a separate or mirrored screen.

Change sidecar options

After setting up your iPad as a secondary screen for your MacBook Air, you can make changes to the options in the Display settings.

❖ Select Apple menu ⬚ > Systems Setting, then click on the Display ⬚ button on the side bar. (You might have to scroll down.)
❖ Select your iPad's name on the right side of the window, then carry out any of the below:

> Click on the **Use as** drop-down menu, and then select one of the options. You can use your iPad as the main screen, mirrored screen or extended screen.
> Click on the drop-down menu beside Show Sidebar then choose one of the options.
> Activate **Enable double tap on Apple Pencil**

Use Sidecar

❖ Carry out any of the below:

> Move a window from your MacBook to your iPad: Drag the window to the edge of your display till the cursor is visible on the iPad. Or while making use of an application, select Window> Move to iPad.

> Move a window from your iPad to your MacBook: Drag the window to the edge of your display till the cursor is visible on the MacBook. Or while making use of an application, select Window> Move to Mac.

> Use the sidebar on your iPad: Use your Apple pencil or finger to touch icons in the side bar to hide ⬇ or display ⬆ the Dock, hide ⬆ or display ⬇ the menu bar, or display the keyboard ⌨ on your screen.

> Switch between your MacBook desktop & your iPad on iPad: Use one of your fingers to swipe up from the lower edge of your iPad to reveal the Home Screen. Swipe up & hold to reveal your iPad's Dock. Swipe up & hold in the middle of your display to reveal the Application Switcher. To go back to your MacBook desktop, swipe up and then touch the Continuity button ▣ .

❖ When you want to stop making use of your iPad, touch the Disconnect button  in the lower part of the side bar on your iPad.
To disconnect on your MacBook, simply click on the active iPad displayed in the Screen Mirroring menu in the menu bar.

Use your iPhone as a webcam on your MacBook

Get Started

Before using the Continuity Camera feature, you must:

- ❖ Ensure your MacBook is running the latest version of macOS Ventura and your iPhone is running the latest version of iOS 16.
- ❖ Make sure your MacBook Air & your iPhone are using the same Apple ID
- ❖ Make sure you activate Bluetooth & Wifi on your MacBook Air & your iPhone
- ❖ Mount your iPhone

Mount your iPhone

Mount your iPhone with any iPhone-compatible mounts & stands. After mounting your iPhone, make sure your phone is:

- ❖ Close to your MacBook Air
- ❖ Stable
- ❖ Locked
- ❖ Set in a way that its back cameras are facing you & unobstructed

Select an external camera on your Mac

- ❖ Use a cable to connect the device to your Mac or connect it wirelessly.
- ❖ Launch an application that captures video, and then carry out any of the below:
  - ➢ Face-Time: Click on the **Video** button in the menus bar, then select your iPhone or the Camera.
  - ➢ Photos booth: Click on the **Camera** button in the menus bar, then select your iPhone or a camera.
  - ➢ QuickTime Player: Select File, click on New Movie Recording, hover over the window, click on the down arrow $\vee$, then select one of the cameras.
  - ➢ 3rd-party applications: You can use your iPhone or external camera with 3rd-party applications that you downloaded from the Apps Store. To learn how simply go through the developer's manual.

Use your iPhone as a microphone or webcam

❖ Open an application on your MacBook Air that has access to the Mic or camera, such as FaceTime.
❖ Follow the directives above to select your iPhone as the Mic or camera in the applications' settings or menu bar.
❖ You can carry out any of the below:
  ➢ Pause the audio or video: Touch the **Pause** button on your phone, or unlock your phone.
  ➢ Resume the audio or video: Touch the **Resume** button on your phone or lock your iPhone.
  ➢ Stop making use of your phone as a Mic or webcam: Quit the application on your MacBook Air.
  ➢ Remove your phone as one of the webcam options: Touch the **Disconnect** button on your iPhone.
  To reconnect your phone, use a USB cable to connect your phone to your MacBook.

Activate Video Effects

After using your phone as your MacBook's webcam, you can click on the Controls Centre 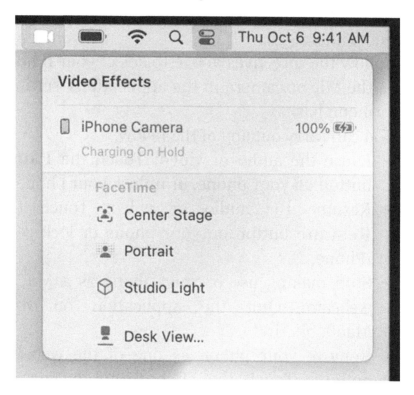 icon in the menu bar on your MacBook Air, and then click on **Video Effects** to add any of the effects below:

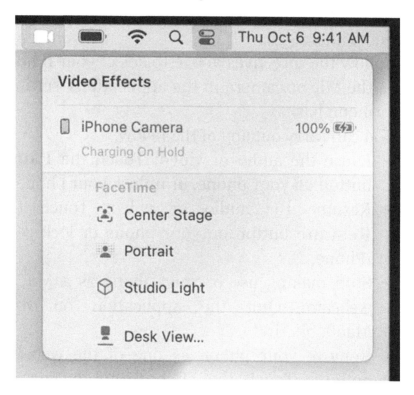

❖ Centre stage: This feature makes sure you remain in the frame while moving around.
❖ Portrait mode.
❖ Studio Light: Makes the background dimmer & brightens your face.

❖ Desk View: Displays the top view of your table and your face together.

If you can't find your phone as a Mic or camera option

If you can't find your phone in the Mic or camera list in an application or Sounds setting, try the following.

❖ Use a USB cable to connect your phone to your MacBook Air & check once more.
❖ Check the following:
  ➢ Your MacBook is running the latest version of macOS Ventura and your iPhone is running the latest version of iOS 16.
  ➢ You've activated Continuity Camera Webcam on your iPhone in the Settings application> General > AirPlay and Hand-off.
  ➢ Your phone recognizes the MacBook Air as a trusted device.
  ➢ You've activated Bluetooth & WiFi on your iPhone & MacBook Air
  ➢ Both devices are using the same Apple ID
  ➢ Both devices are within Bluetooth range (thirty feet)

> The video application you are using has been updated to the latest version

Upload pictures & scans with Continuity Camera

The Continuity Camera feature allows you to capture a photo or scan a document with a nearby iPad or iPhone & have the picture or scanned document appear instantly on your MacBook Air exactly where it's needed, such as in an e-mail, document, folder, or note.

To use the Continuity Camera feature, you have to activate Bluetooth, & Wifi on both devices. You must also ensure that both devices are using the same Apple ID.

The following applications support Continuity Camera on your MacBook Air:

- ❖ TextEdit
- ❖ Pages
- ❖ Numbers
- ❖ Notes
- ❖ Message
- ❖ Mail
- ❖ Keynote
- ❖ Finder.

Capture a picture

- ❖ Launch an application that supports Continuity Camera on your MacBook Air.
- ❖ Do one of the following actions:
  - ➢ Ctrl-click where you want to place the picture in the application window. From the shortcut

menu that pops-up, select Insert from iPad or iPhone> Take Photos.

➢ From the File menu (or the Insert menu), select Insert from iPad or iPhone> Take Photos.

❖ Launch the Camera application on your iPad or iPhone. Touch the Capture button ⬤ to snap a picture, and then touch the **Use Photo** button. Your picture will appear in the window on your MacBook Air.

Scan documents

❖ Launch an application that supports Continuity Camera on your MacBook Air.
❖ Do one of the following actions:
  ➢ Ctrl-click where you want to place the picture in the application window. From the shortcut menu that pops-up, select Insert from iPad or iPhone> Scan Document.
  ➢ From the File menu (or the Insert menu), select Insert from iPad or iPhone> Scan Document.

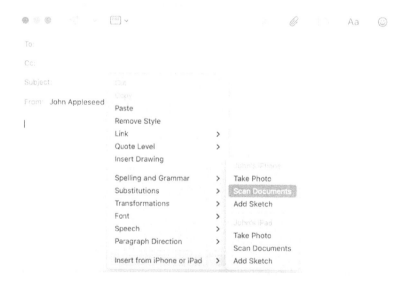

❖ Launch the Camera application on your iPad or iPhone. Position your phone in a way that the document can be seen clearly on your screen & wait for the scan to finish. To capture a scan manually, touch the Capture button , drag the edges to adjust the scan, and then touch the **Keep Scan** button.

❖ Touch the **Save** button when you are done. Your scan will appear in a PDF format in the window on your MacBook Air

AirDrop

AirDrop allows you to send pictures, webpages, documents, etc. to an iPad, iPhone or Mac that's close to your device.

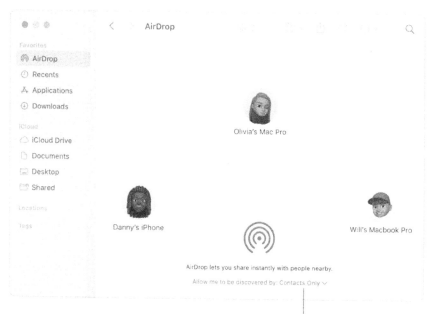

Control who can send items to you.

Send items via AirDrop

❖ From a Finder window or the desktop: Ctrl-click on the item you plan on sending, select the **Share** button from the menu, select AirDrop, and then choose the device you plan on sending the item to.

❖ From the Finder: Click on the **AirDrop** button in the Finder side bar, and then drag the item to the device you plan on sending the item to.

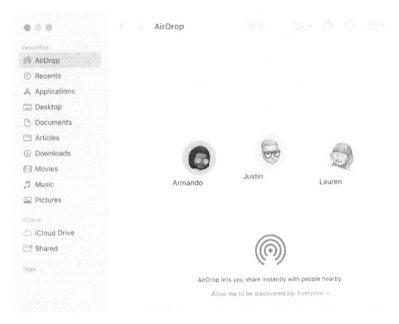

❖ From an application: Click on the Share icon in the application's tool bar, select the **AirDrop**

button, and then choose the device you plan on sending the item to.

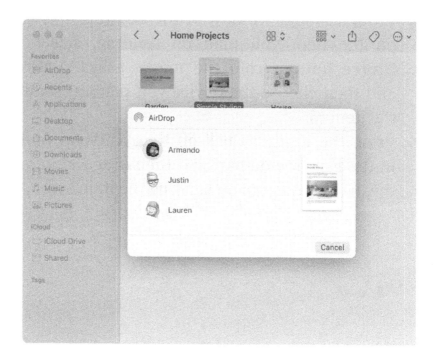

Get things using AirDrop

When somebody sends an item to your MacBook Air via AirDrop, you can choose to accept & store it.

❖ In the AirDrop notification on your MacBook, click on Accept, and then select one of the options.

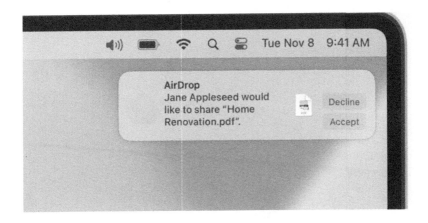

❖ Find the item in the Downloads folder or the application you stored the file in.

Let others send things to your MacBook via AirDrop

❖ Click on the Finder icon 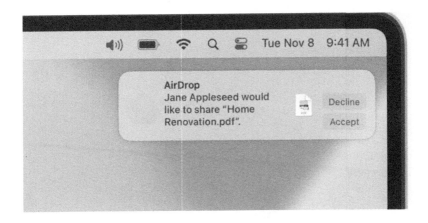 in the Dock to launch the Finder window.
❖ Click on the **AirDrop** button in the Finder side bar.
❖ In the AirDrop window, click on the "Allow me to be found by" drop-down menu and then select one of the options.

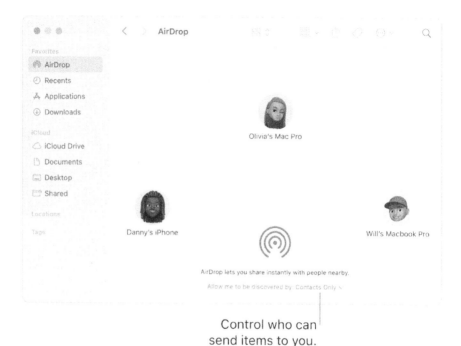

Olivia's Mac Pro

Danny's iPhone

Will's Macbook Pro

AirDrop lets you share instantly with people nearby.

Allow me to be discovered by: Contacts Only

Control who can
send items to you.

Use Control Centre to manage AirDrop

Use the Controls Centre to quickly activate or deactivate AirDrop & select who can send files to you.

Click on the Controls Centre icon in the menu bar, then carry out any of the below:

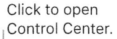
Click to open
Control Center.

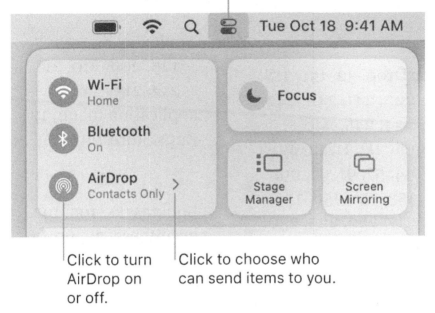

Click to turn
AirDrop on
or off.

Click to choose who
can send items to you.

❖ Activate or deactivate AirDrop: click on the
   AirDrops button.
❖ To select who can send files to you via AirDrop,
   click on the arrow beside AirDrop, then click on
   Everybody or Only Contacts

INDEX

A

AirDrop, 32, 151, 218, 222, 241, 242, 243, 244, 245, 246

Apple ID, 11, 12, 43, 44, 57, 91, 97, 99, 153, 156, 158, 159, 217, 222, 225, 230, 234, 236

Apple menu, 10, 12, 14, 17, 18, 20, 25, 33, 35, 50, 51, 52, 55, 58, 65, 66, 67, 68, 70, 81, 85, 86, 87, 88, 90, 92, 95, 96, 101, 102, 103, 105, 107, 113, 120, 123, 124, 128, 129, 133, 134, 136, 137, 138, 143, 146, 173, 177, 209, 212, 213, 218, 222, 225, 226

Apple Pay, 6, 14, 127, 128, 209, 210, 211, 212, 213

application menu, 17

Apps Store, 231

B

Bookmarks, 195, 197

brightness, 32, 65, 66, 67, 141

C

camera, 231, 234

Camera, 93, 107, 169, 230, 231, 235, 236, 237, 239

Continuity Camera, 234

Controls Centre, 10, 16, 30, 32, 33, 34, 68, 85, 121, 136, 174, 175, 226, 233, 245

D

Dark Mode, 82, 85

Dock, 18, 20, 22, 23,
    24, 25, 26, 27, 35,
    41, 69, 70, 72, 76,
    78, 84, 112, 114, 120,
    124, 160, 219, 221,
    228, 244

E

e-mail, 11, 30, 61, 64,
    116, 117, 156, 157,
    159, 180, 181, 183,
    185, 186, 188, 189,
    190, 192, 202, 203,
    213, 217, 236
Ethernet, 9, 52, 55, 56,
    57

F

FaceTime, 153, 154,
    155, 157, 158, 159,
    160, 161, 162, 164,
    165, 167, 168, 169,
    170, 171, 172, 173,
    174, 175, 176, 177,
    178, 179, 232
Finder, 20, 21, 22, 59,
    64, 70, 106, 107, 111,

112, 148, 150, 151,
    152, 236, 242, 244

H

Handoff, 217, 218, 219,
    220, 222, 223
hot corners, 112

I

iCloud, 11, 12, 20, 44,
    151, 180, 218, 223

K

keyboard shortcuts, 61,
    64, 140, 141, 142,
    146, 147, 179

L

language, 8, 100, 101,
    102, 135, 201
Launchpad, 23, 40, 41,
    42, 48, 62, 69
Live Text, 115, 116, 202

M

Mail, 70, 73, 104, 180,
    181, 183, 184, 185,

186, 191, 192, 217, 236

Memoji, 91, 92, 99, 100

menu bar, 9, 15, 16, 17, 19, 30, 32, 34, 53, 54, 57, 64, 65, 68, 70, 72, 76, 78, 84, 85, 121, 123, 136, 164, 170, 171, 174, 175, 226, 228, 229, 232, 233, 245

Mission Control, 27, 80, 141

N

network, 9, 16, 53, 54, 55

Night Shift, 85, 86, 87

P

passcode, 9, 11, 43, 54, 55, 90, 96, 97, 98, 99, 128, 130, 131

Q

Quick Look, 59, 60, 61

Quick Note, 112, 118

R

Restart, 51

S

Safari, 70, 104, 129, 193, 194, 195, 198, 199, 200, 201, 202, 203, 204, 205, 207, 208, 209, 217

screen saver, 87, 88, 89, 90

Screenshot, 61, 62, 65

Shut Down, 50

Sidecar, 224, 225, 226, 227

Siri, 13, 69, 132, 133, 134, 135, 136, 137, 138, 139

software update, 38

Split View, 76, 78

Spotlight, 16, 38, 39, 70, 133, 137, 138

Stacks, 110, 111

Stage Manager, 119, 120, 121, 122, 123, 124, 125
System Settings, 10, 35, 37, 87, 95

T

tabs, 73, 197, 198
text size, 104, 105
Touch ID, 5, 6, 14, 127, 128, 129, 131, 209, 211
Trackpad, 46, 48

U

Universal Clipboard, 221, 222, 223
USB, 4, 55, 58, 232, 234

V

volume, 32, 67, 68, 138, 150, 172, 173

W

Wallpaper, 81, 83, 84
webcam, 232, 233
WiFi, 9, 16, 32, 52, 53, 54, 57, 234

Made in the USA
Las Vegas, NV
15 January 2024

84347254R10144